"Greg Sarris's resonant memoir explores identities, heritages, and the legacies of places. [. . .] Testifying to the impacts of people on the land, the powerful memoir *Becoming Story* lauds the power of language when it comes to leaving tracks for others to follow."

—*Foreword Reviews*

"Sarris's Northern California landscapes are sacred texts, peopled with elk, pronghorn, osprey, and lizards. Traversing different lives, *Becoming Story* is a heartfelt contemplation of one man's decades-long journey of returning home."

—*San Francisco Book Review*

"In this powerful memoir-in-essays, Greg Sarris explores questions about home, connection, and belonging in vivid prose that is both humorous and profound."

—**LAURA SCHMITT**, *Electric Literature*

"In Sarris's latest work, *Becoming Story*, he invites us into an intimate and communal California Indian world. Part memoir, part history, part ethnography, the work has echoes of Momaday's *The Way to Rainy Mountain*. He shares, with refreshing honesty, his family roots—their depths and dislocations, as well as their strong sinews that the forces of settler colonialism and American genocide could not sever. His narrative reminds us that the roots of our tribal identities 'remember' and, ultimately, restore(y) us."

—**THERESA GREGOR**, Professor of American Indian Studies

BECOMING STORY

BECOMING STORY

A Journey among Seasons, Places, Trees, and Ancestors

GREG SARRIS

HEYDAY
50

Berkeley, California

The Library of Congress has cataloged the hardcover edition as follows:
Names: Sarris, Greg, author.
Title: Becoming story : a journey among seasons, places, trees, and
    ancestors / Greg Sarris.
Other titles: Journey among seasons, places, trees, and ancestors
Description: Berkeley, California : Heyday, [2022]
Identifiers: LCCN 2021036078 (print) | LCCN 2021036079 (ebook) | ISBN
    9781597145671 (hardcover) | ISBN 9781597145688 (epub)
Subjects: LCSH: Sarris, Greg. | Miwok Indians--California--Sonoma
    County--Biography. | Sonoma County (Calif.)--Biography. | Miwok
    Indians--Folklore.
Classification: LCC E99.M69 S37 2022 (print) | LCC E99.M69 (ebook) | DDC
    979.4/18--dc23/eng/20211020
LC record available at https://lccn.loc.gov/2021036078
LC ebook record available at https://lccn.loc.gov/2021036079

Cover Art: Adobe Stock/Elena Kozyreva
Cover Design: Archie Ferguson
Interior Design/Typesetting: Ashley Ingram

Published by Heyday
P.O. Box 9145, Berkeley, California 94709
(510) 549-3564
heydaybooks.com

Printed in East Peoria, Illinois, by Versa Press, Inc.

10 9 8 7 6 5 4 3 2 1

CONTENTS

SEASONS

FROST

Winter.

Not ancient stories about the time, before this one, when the animals were still people, before Coyote messed things up with his hapless machinations. Nor the dark room, warm but still black as the cold midwinter night outside, with nothing but the floating voice of the storyteller impersonating the people in the stories: crafty Coyote's devious whispering; Blue Jay's shrill admonishments; Frog's old-man rasp; Quail, the most beautiful of all the people, her gentle-as-brook-water songs. None of those things. But cows—feeding the cows, their cloven hooves planted in the frost-covered earth, nostrils blowing steam above an unfastened bale of alfalfa.

I would stand, warming my hands in my coat pockets, for hours watching the cows. I had a good eye then, not just for an old cow's swollen knee, or maybe a rheumy eye, but even the faintest rise in her hide, indicating the presence of a grub.

And the alfalfa, too: it was best if you could see dried purple flowers, sign of an early June harvest, after just enough warm weather. I was seven. I had no cows of my own but followed the local dairyman. I wanted a cow.

No Indians at home either. I was adopted. At the time, I knew nothing of my birth father, Emilio Hilario, or my Coast Miwok heritage. That would come twenty years down the road. And I would hear about the things the old-timers did. Winter activities; storytelling, for instance. Renowned Pomo basket weaver and doctor Mabel McKay, who I was fortunate to have known, explained the rules about the ancient-time stories: "Only tell them in winter, after the first frost and before the last frost. Think about them then, their meanings. Not in summer, when there's snakes and things in the grass and you need to pay attention to where you are going." But that has nothing to do with memory, what surfaces from experience, as I recall winter now.

There was a man named Tommy Baca. He had only one arm, and he was a housepainter. My mother said a thousand times no one could mix color like Tommy Baca. He was a stocky man of medium height, with a broad, handsome face. He had thick, wavy black hair. He smiled a lot. I marveled at how he kept papers and such tucked against his side, just below his armpit, with the stub of his missing arm, and the way the stub would move, seemingly of its own volition, when he was excited, though I was careful not to let him find me looking. "Don't stare at people," my mother snapped. He was Indian, Coast Miwok; if I knew as much then, I don't remember, and certainly not the Coast Miwok part. What interested me was that he had cows.

And because my parents were friends with him, I had access to the cows. They were steers, actually; mixed-blood dairy calves, Guernsey and Hereford, which in those days you could get for a drop in the bucket, as the dairy farmers kept only their purebred heifers. Out at Tommy's place, west of town, I could spend hours with the critters. Once his son, Mark, about seven, like me, asked, "Why do you always look at Dad's cows?" and I felt as if it was a bad thing, like when other kids called me "adopted."

I'm not clear about this next part. What happened exactly. Maybe because for a month or more I was on cloud nine. Did I hear my parents and Tommy Baca talking in the kitchen after work one night? Did I hear about it that way, before the afternoon out at Tommy's when he said, "Pick out the one you want. Take your pick"?

A Guernsey and Hereford crossbreed steer. I kept him in

the field adjacent my parents' house. I named him Harry. Why I picked him from a lot of half a dozen others exactly like him, I don't know, or remember. He proved intelligent. He knew the time of day, precisely, when I arrived home from school, and never failed to stand just inside the aluminum gate— always the same spot—waiting for me. He learned to genuflect, lowering himself on one knee, so that you could scratch the crown of his head and, later, when he grew, to make it easier to climb aboard his back. Yes, we rode him—every kid from the neighborhood in those days has a picture of himself or herself astride Harry.

His horns grew, but he was gentle, careful even, when he tossed his head to shoo flies or strew a flake of hay over the ground. Well, there was that one time, head lowered, when he charged Alan Chaney, chasing him out of the field. But no one cared since everyone knew Alan was a bully and had no doubt provoked Harry.

That was so long ago. A million stories ago. Of course, I found out who my father was, and now I can look back and understand things I hadn't the faintest idea of before. The connections between me and Tommy Baca, for instance. His grandmother, Maria Copa, sang for my great-great-grandfather, Tom Smith, the renowned last Coast Miwok medicine man, as he doctored the sick. I can imagine them along the coast and through inland valleys, traveling in a wagon and later in a Model T Ford. That box with the stuff of history spills— the ancient villages fall out: Olumpali and Alaguali for Maria Copa, and Petaluma and Olemitcha for Tom Smith; then the Spanish galleons and English steamers, oceans crossed, wars, marriages, priests and soldiers, adobe and brick, overalls and Panama hats and, still, clamshell disc beads and flicker feathers—and I see in that chance meeting of an adopted boy and a one-armed housepainter the miraculous web that is all of time, nothing more, nothing less, all-inclusive. But it's memory that prevails still. Memory trounces this miraculous web—that is, if memory is not the vantage point from which I gaze upon it. No, not even Grandpa Tom's songs left on wax cylinders, or his ancient-time stories left in a graduate student's dissertation; not beads and feathers. Winter. It's feeding the cows—feeding Harry. And frost. The earth is blanketed with frost. A quarter-inch thick at least, on the bare tree limbs, on rocks. Harry too is covered, topped as if with a layer of frosting. Harry steps into the sun to munch the alfalfa I just tossed over the fence, and I see the frost so cold, so powerful, begin to fall from his back, barely perceptible, trifling dust. And, again, I'm not sure what happened exactly—whether I had overheard "fattened" and "spring grass" in a conversation between my parents and Tommy Baca the night before, or months before, and didn't understand, or chose not to—but at that moment I got it, understood the whole story, what the words would mean after the last frost, come summer. I might protest, but it would do no good. Never mind the purple blooms in the alfalfa. What a complicated and frightening world replaces winter.

IRIS

Spring.

Mabel McKay, she told me about this, too. Spring. "Coming-out time," she said. Which was how the season was described, quite literally, by many Native California cultures. New growth, blossoms, sedge sprouting on creek banks—when, after winter, it is no longer safe to tell stories, not only because you must pay attention to where you are going, watchful for snakes and such, but because you too are coming out, becoming story. Living again; living new. Tribes had ceremonies to mark the season. Often every plant and tree was named—every creature, even—lest the people forget it, and it, in turn, forgets the people. Mabel recalled the *sectu*, or ceremonial leader, in Colusa standing atop the Roundhouse entrance at dawn one spring morning, facing east, announcing each part of Creation, as if in that faint light the world itself was emerging for the first time.

I remember Eileen (not her real name). Spring, the miracle of continuation; yes, it's Eileen I see. She had relatives on the Kashaya Pomo reservation, and she took me there once to the Strawberry Festival, a ceremony to dedicate the new fruits. This was where I first saw Essie Parrish, the great Kashaya Pomo prophet, a big woman in ceremonial dress—traditional long skirt and clamshell disc bead necklace—praying in her language before a table crowded with food, the least of which were the tin pots and Indian baskets heaped full of bright red strawberries. "She's saying something about spring, Indian things," Eileen attempted to translate, though she didn't know the language either. For the Kashaya Pomo, the wild strawberry was the first fruit of the New Year, and therefore was symbolic of spring. The ceremony—the costumes, songs, four nights of dancing that preceded the feast—came from Essie Parrish's Dream. Did Eileen know that? I certainly didn't.

That was forty years ago, at least. I didn't know anything then. That I was Indian. That Eileen was my cousin. I know about my Coast Miwok heritage now, but it's been a long journey. I'm now chairman of my tribe, the Federated Indians of Graton Rancheria. We are Coast Miwok and Southern Pomo, descendants of a handful of survivors from Marin and southern Sonoma Counties. We struggle to start anew a spring tradition. We offer prayers in languages we are relearning; we listen to songs found on wax cylinders in museums and university libraries. I've learned some history. And always there's Mabel, since deceased, whose advice I nonetheless never forget. Yet it's Eileen I recall now—but not because she took me to the Strawberry Festival, my first so-called Indian ceremony. Frankly, I didn't think much about it. No, what comes out new, magic to the eye, is a story, and it starts with Eileen.

Simple enough—I had a crush on her. I'd see her in first hall, not far from my locker, talking with her sister, friends. Heaps of black hair. Eyeliner and lipstick, a mole planted with a brow pencil above the corner of her mouth. She was a woman. She wore tight black skirts—girls had to wear dresses to school in those days—and colorful silky blouses. She offered her friends only a meager nod, a half-tilt of the chin, the tough-girl greeting— no phony smiles, no popular-girl routine. I didn't have a chance. I wasn't a tough guy. Anyone remember them—the guys in skin-tight 401s and white T-shirts, one sleeve rolled up holding a soft pack of Camels above a bulging and, if you were *really* a tough guy, tattooed bicep? I was a late bloomer: flat-limbed and soft-faced; fourteen but looking like a twelve-year-old or, worse, a girl, sporting an oily pompadour. I lived in a middle-class neighborhood. I was also white, and everyone knew the toughest guys were Indian or Mexican. I got the nod from Eileen one day, but what could I say? Ask if she wanted a cigarette? Did I have any cigarettes?

Then, some luck. Ritchie, the guy who sat in front of me in math, was Eileen's cousin. But it wasn't Ritchie who afforded me an introduction. It was Tommy Baca, the one-armed housepainter who had given me, years before, the crossbreed steer I'd named Harry. Tommy Baca was Ritchie's uncle, and Eileen's, which I learned from Ritchie in an unrelated conversation.

So when Eileen nodded at me, I told her I knew her cousin. She narrowed her eyes, sizing me up, I figured. Had she really given me a no, or had I imagined as much? My stomach was in knots. What if one of her friends came along and caught her talking to this gangly kid? Would she say something to humiliate me?

"Ritchie?" she finally said. Her mouth barely moved, as if even the name of her cousin she intended to keep to herself.

I told her no and mentioned Tommy's son, Mark, which caught her off guard, and then I launched into a pathetic story about Harry, who had ended up on dinner plates in the Saddle and Sirloin restaurant.

She offered the faintest smile. At lunch later that day she

handed me a note folded eight times into a hard square: "You are my friend. L."

We walked the halls after that, sat together at lunch time. I learned who she liked and who she didn't. Which girls she wanted to "kick their asses." I met her sister, her friends. I met tough people, the *really* tough people. Everything changed. People looked at me differently. The hoods noticed me. Teachers glared with reproach, and some confusion. The most noticeable reactions came from kids in my neighborhood, since my association with Eileen violated social and racial codes. I was a white-looking kid hanging out with an Indian girl. I now had enemies. "Greaser," "spic-lover" (as if Eileen were Mexican)—I heard those names. The week before Christmas vacation, a kid named Steve, whose father owned a plumbing company, knocked me to the ground. I fought back, despite the fact that he was older and nearly twice my size. I came to school the next day with a black eye, sort of, and definitely a split lip. Two of Eileen's friends, older, one a high school dropout, found Steve on his way home from school alone and, as Eileen reported to me, "beat him until he was crying like a baby."

Eileen and I walked uptown, too. We spent hours after school and on Saturdays walking. We looked in storefront windows, made fun of the mannequins in Rosenberg's Department Store, and of anyone on the street, particularly women affecting airs, aloof like the mannequins pointing in one direction with stiff plastic fingers while gazing to the heavens with glass eyes. We followed Fourth Street, Santa Rosa's main drag, from the old train station at one end, just past a string of pawn shops and the Silver Dollar, a corner dive with black-painted dollar signs embossed on the saloon-style swinging front doors, back up to Rosenberg's and farther on to the Flamingo Hotel, which marked the other end of Fourth Street with its revolving neon flamingo atop a freestanding sixty-foot tower. We rested in Old Courthouse Square, sat close together on a bench. Unsure of what to do at this juncture—at least *I* was unsure of what to do, as if this were the next step in a ritual that had begun with the walking—we just continued talking about people, passersby. This one walked like a duck, that one's socks were different colors.

"I used to think they were married," Eileen said one day after school, and then laughed at herself.

I hadn't been watching, but when I looked, I saw two old Indians, sixty plus, him in a thick overcoat and fedora, her in a house-dress and scarf, making their way up the street. It was getting late, the streetlights already on, and the pair seemed to have appeared from the darkness behind them, coming slowly into the light of the square. They seemed unaware of one another, or of anyone else, gazing at everything and nothing at the same time, as if they were lost, two old people in a strange city, or children abandoned at a fair. They stopped at the corner, and after the light changed and they crossed the street, they were gone, into the darkness, just as they had come.

"Yeah, looks like it," I said, not sure what else to say.

The woman was Eileen's friend's grandmother; the old man was her brother. I'd met the friend while hanging out with Eileen and often visited his house, a small place behind the fairgrounds, where the old man—Uncle, they called him— sat on the front porch dressed, even on hot Santa Rosa afternoons, in the same pleated overcoat and fedora. He was a big man, heavyset and solid. He could do anything, the friend said—Uncle was an Indian doctor. He pulled a bird's leg bone out of his sister's eye once. He could see the future by holding hot coals in his hands. One day, a bunch of us piled into a car, leaving Uncle in his aluminum folding chair on the front porch, and then there he was again minutes later, two miles uptown on a bench in the square, waving to us as we stopped for a red light—I saw that. "Uncle's got wings," someone whispered when the light changed.

Mabel told me, many years later, that Uncle was the last of the old-time doctors, trained here on the earth. They followed a strict regimen of abstinence from meat and sexual relations. "Lots of rules," Mabel said. And, yes, they could do stupendous things, like traveling as fast as a hummingbird. In fact, Uncle spooked Mabel once. She was with Essie Parrish, the two of them enjoying a soda at the counter in Thrifty's, when Uncle, overcoat and fedora, appeared outside the window. Attempting to escape him, the two frightened ladies boarded a bus, only to find him at the other end of town, waiting for them when they got off. "Playing with us," Mabel chuckled.

When my friend told me the stories about Uncle, even after the incident I had personally witnessed in the square, I said nothing. It felt like none of my business, and if I were to ask questions, it would only highlight the fact that I was an outsider. If Eileen had heard similar things, still it was not my business to remark or ask questions—she was an Indian and I was not. I kept thinking about Uncle and his sister, though. What of the manner in which the two of them had appeared just then, out of nowhere, walking with the measured steps of old people, yet somehow effortlessly gliding—or was I only imagining as much because of what I had witnessed and the stories I had heard? Where were they off to on a cold winter's evening?

It seems funny now when I think of those junior high school days. As I learned later, Eileen's father and my father were second cousins, something like that, a grandson and a great-grandson of Tom Smith, the famous (sometimes infamous) Coast Miwok Indian doctor known as much for his supernatural feats—which included causing the 1906 earthquake—as for his many wives. Was he something of an "earth doctor" like Uncle? Seems he didn't abstain from sexual relations; he had over twenty children. One of his wives, Eileen's great-grandmother, was Kashaya Pomo from the Haupt Ranch in northern Sonoma County; another, my great-great-grandmother, was Coast Miwok from Tomales Bay in Marin County.

Through the trick and circumstance of history, I now had a crush on Eileen. One generation, and the connection had been broken. We were complete strangers. I was white and lost in her world. I was adopted, and rumor had it that my natural father might be Mexican, a mantra I repeated to Eileen. Never mind that with blue eyes, fair skin, and coming from a good part of town, I was white. Eileen was Indian, and her mother was Indian too, Coast Miwok, in fact the granddaughter of Maria Copa, who not only assisted Tom Smith doctoring the sick but, with him, helped a UC Berkeley graduate student in the 1930s compile descriptions of Coast Miwok traditions and a vocabulary. Spring activities, spring traditions—the history Eileen and I share, which I think of now.

I also think of Tom Smith. From pictures I have seen, he was a stout man, broad-faced with heavy, you might say weary, eyes; in one picture in which he is standing, it looks as if his left leg is slightly bowed. I imagine him atop his Roundhouse on Jenner Point, above the wide mouth of the Russian River, facing east to the first light of day, visible above the jagged line of hills. Naming oaks, buckeyes, berries, clovers, willow, peppergrass, angelica; and animals, too, and birds. Maria Copa was there. She heard the names of things. She watched the river find itself in that light, twist and lengthen to the sea. Paths everywhere . . . There were lots of coming-out ceremonies then, songs for after a girl's first menses, new-woman songs, and also the secret cults, the songs and arduous tasks, whereby a boy becomes a man.

I had to kiss Eileen. It was expected. Enough walking, enough talking. I wanted to kiss her. I planned to make my move on a Saturday night. Did tough guys plan such things? Us kids hung out inside an abandoned garage at the end of Sixth Street, just below the newly constructed 101 Freeway. It was next to Randy's house. Randy was white but real tough. His sister knew Hells Angels; his father tended bar at the

Silver Dollar, two blocks away; and his mother, who drank at the bar, often grew impatient waiting for his father and wandered home, where she'd push up the kitchen window and holler hoarse-voiced for Randy to "come down outta there," meaning the second floor of the garage. Each time I heard her, I remembered the story of how she once struck one of Randy's friends with a hammer. We had a transistor radio up there, a table and chairs, and mattresses placed strategically in dark corners. I was even thinking about which mattress we'd end up on, which side of the room.

I went to her house first, as if, at fourteen, I had arrived to escort her to a formal dinner or something. We sat on the couch, a respectable distance apart. At one point, her mother came into the room, and then, without acknowledging me, without saying a word to either of us, returned to the kitchen, where she was playing cards with a couple of her sisters, Eileen's aunts. Eileen said her mother knew my father, my adoptive father. I was excited: apparently, Eileen had talked to her mother about me. I told Eileen my parents were divorced now, my mother was working at JCPenney to help support the family. I thought the family hard luck would impress Eileen. "My father, all he did was drink," I said. Then I overheard her mother in the kitchen say something about "big eyes." Did she mean me? Was I being nosey? Is that what her mother thought of me?

It was the end of February then, maybe the beginning of March. It was cold outside. We walked in the dark, under a canopy of bushy trees that lined the street. Upstairs, in Randy's garage, it wasn't any warmer, and the two candles, upright in coffee mugs, didn't give much light either. We sat at the table with the others—Randy and his girlfriend, plus two Mexican guys and a Mexican girl—and talked in hushed voices. A song played on the transistor. Randy smoked. He talked about the end of the world: a friend of his mother's had read a prophecy in the Bible and determined, from certain current events, that the world would end at twelve o'clock on New Year's the following year. Randy talked a lot about the end of the world up there, and so we did too. I would be fifteen when the world ended. I heard voices in one corner, on a mattress, but didn't dare look to see, or ask, who it was—I didn't want to be nosey. It was freezing. I was holding Eileen's hand. Eileen finished a cigarette, rubbing it out in the ashtray with her free hand, then said she was still cold, which I took as my cue: now we must head to a mattress. Which one? I couldn't stand up and have a discussion about it. I was supposed to know. I let go of her hand and took hold of her elbow, securing her arm, without knowing where I was going to lead her—should I ask first if she wanted to go to a mattress?—when, all at once, I heard Randy's mother. I was distracted, consumed with worry over my predicament with Eileen, and it wasn't until I heard "shits" and "sons of bitches," and saw the swirl of commotion as everyone was fleeing the table, that I understood Randy's mother wasn't inside the house next door but at the bottom of the stairs. Then I heard her on the stairs.

Eileen was already gone. I was alone at the table. I turned, walked two steps to the window, and jumped. Not two floors down but onto the freeway embankment—the garage was that close. I'd seen other kids jump; still, I felt brave. I climbed onto the freeway, into the bright lights and whir of traffic. It was what, ten o'clock, and the freeway, even in a then-much-quieter Northern California, was busy. I flew to the center divider, and then, when it was clear, tore the rest of the way across and came back down the other side to the safer, better-lighted part of town.

I debated whether or not to go back. Most everyone would be scattered. Truth was, I was afraid to encounter Randy's mother. I thought of Eileen. She probably went home. I told myself I had missed my chance. But I was confident I would have another opportunity. Didn't we both know that? I told myself that, the next time, things would go smoothly. I pictured us going to the mattress, my hand still clutching her elbow, but by then I was already heading over to Fourth Street, going home.

On Saturday nights, Fourth Street was crowded with flashy cars filled with teenagers who hurled insults as well as flirtations from open windows—old-style cruising. I found the wide street more congested than usual, however. Cars were stopped, moving only at a snail's pace when they did move. The sidewalks were bustling, not just with the regular Saturday-night teenagers leaning against their parked cars but with folks of all ages, families even, mothers and fathers with kids in hand. I had crossed town earlier following College Avenue, five blocks away, and totally missed the busy scene. Old Courthouse Square was jammed. There I saw folks collected before antique cars—Model T's, Packards—that lined the square on both sides, and I understood immediately the reason for the hubbub: a car show on display the entire weekend, apparently. Never mind the cold weather and rambunctious teenagers, people wanted to see the cars.

I kept on my way, passing the square. I'd had enough for the night. I was in front of Rosenberg's when I heard the jeer. Something about "get you" from out of the racket of car radios and idling engines. I paid no attention. Then I saw a reflection in the storefront window: a face framed, as if in a square box, coming out at me. When I turned, I saw it was Steve, the guy who had beat me up, hanging out of a car window.

"You're dead, punk."

I froze; in fact, the whole world froze—Steve, the car, everything as still as the mannequin in the window next to me. There was still the din of engines and music above the line of cars, and perhaps it was that disembodied noise that brought me back to my senses: I thought to run.

There were other guys in the car with Steve. He could've gotten out of the car then—he was in the front passenger seat and the car was stopped in traffic—but for whatever reason he didn't. By the time I realized that, I was already a good ways down the block. I turned for the first time to look and found that no one was chasing me. But the car had its turn signal on, and I figured Steve and his friends would come back around the block for me. The car was inching closer to the intersection. I scrambled onto a side street, around a corner, nearly careening into Uncle and his sister approaching Fourth Street. They were walking in the same aloof, haphazard manner as before. Uncle was wearing his overcoat and fedora, and his sister was bundled in a heavy overcoat, perhaps an extra layer of scarves—I wasn't looking closely. I do know the old woman hissed with admonishment, as if I were a reckless kid who'd actually smashed into her, and Uncle made grunting sounds, which I took, in the moment I heard him, as a sign of irritation also. They were in front of an alley. I cut down the dark path and dove behind a row of garbage cans.

I didn't look back or up. Tires screeched in the distance, horns. I crouched in the dirt, as comfortable as possible. Ten minutes later headlights shone at the start of the alley. The car rolled toward the garbage cans and stopped. Was I a magnet for my own doom? I didn't think Steve was able to see where I'd gone; certainly he couldn't have seen me go into the alley once I was off of Fourth Street, much less hide behind these particular garbage cans. Stay or flee? All at once, clunk, a bottle landed squarely in the can next to me. A woman's voice escaped the still-open window, "Not here, James," and the car rolled away.

The next morning, rising late, I found myself outside, alone in an astonishingly warm day. The sun was daffodil yellow. The night had rolled seamlessly into this moment, it seemed. My mother had left for work, my siblings off wherever. Sunday morning. I sat on the curb and lit a cigarette. Across the street, in the neighbor's yard, an iris grew up, rich purple. Flag lilies, people used to call them. Indeed. I went over and smelled the deep inside of the flower, fecund, then sat back down, now facing my mother's house. Right then I was certain I was a tough guy. I could take care of myself. Iris.

The night before, I'd kept hidden an hour, if that. Of course, I'd like to have a story in which Steve found me but I cleverly got away, maybe even fist-fought him and won, or at least stayed out all night, rattled my bones in the cold until the first light of day. As far as I knew, though, Steve and his friends never came close to the alley, if they even bothered looking for me. I don't know; I never again encountered him. I walked home following empty streets.

Maybe it was a confluence of things that made me feel so confident that next morning—the weather, a harbinger of spring, if not a proclamation of its arrival; the cigarette between my fingers; the iris. I ended up kissing Eileen once before she took up with an older, much tougher guy than me. She's gone on with her life now. I'm sitting here remembering all of this.

As it turned out, I would get to know Uncle better, and his sister even better than that. In her later years, before she died at the age of 101, I came to call her Grandma. The family tells me that Uncle and Grandma used to feel sorry for me, that I was always one of their favorites. "Hobo boy," they called me. That night, at the entrance to the alley, I didn't think to imagine they as much as recognized me even. But, if the family is right, might Uncle, in his overcoat and fedora, not have been grunting at me in irritation that night but instead singing a lost boy on his way?

OSPREY

Summer.

Something about the glare of noon. Or nearabouts noon because summertime that hour feels like eternity, the essence of the season itself, halfway between here and there, stopped. Something about the stillness of light, and the motionless surface of the green river. On a dry path above the water even the orange-flowering monkey plant and sticky-leafed mountain balm appear to be waiting, as if for the sun to move again. And then an osprey breaks out of the sky, silver body and black-tipped wings, coursing the snaking path of the river.

All at once, it's the same light, the season again forty years ago, and the girl below the Ferris wheel at the county fair will come along the path with the boy just now heading for the carnival from the livestock barn. She does not know him, wouldn't imagine ever knowing him. But the light is open, empty all around her—never mind the throngs of people, the cotton candy and hot dogs, or the shrieks pouring from the two-story Ferris wheel behind her—and anything is possible. Her friends have gone to toss rings for a stuffed bear. She is alone. She is free.

She sits on a bench and pulls a compact from her purse. She wears a pink-and-black polka-dot blouse with a ruffled front and a black fitted skirt she borrowed from her older sister. She is Indian but she could be Annette Funicello. She could be different. Not like overweight Lynette, whose legs are like stovepipes, or Betty, her other friend, with cat-eye horn-rimmed glasses, poor thing.

She would say it was all like a movie, how, when she looked up, after snapping her purse shut, he was there—her lipstick was on and she looked perfect—and he walked up to her, and he had a car.

She knew better, she would say, too. She wasn't a fool. She was sixteen, after all. She just wasn't thinking. He talked while he drove. He was from Petaluma, on the outskirts. His family had a dairy; he showed cows at the fair, registered Holsteins. That morning, first show, he had won a blue ribbon. It was his lucky day, he said. He'd met Mexican girls before. He liked them. She didn't tell him her name, that it was Eileen, and that her last name was as American as all get-out, but if he had asked and she had told him, he would know she wasn't Mexican, or certainly not all Mexican.

He called the place Wohler Bridge.

She knew it only as the bridge on Eastside Road, the place where Filipinos once held cockfights, big get-togethers where Indian women went to meet those Filipino dandies in pin-striped suits and Panama hats, handling bets and squawking, razor-fitted roosters with equal aplomb. She thought of all this after the boy parked the car and they traversed the dusty parking lot, heading for the trail—how last summer, or the summer before last, her aunts pointed to the place and mentioned these things while driving over the bridge on their way to pick pears someplace.

The boy led the way. Coming around a bend, she saw the monkey plant and mountain balm alongside the path, orange flowers, clumps of sticky leaves. Nothing moved there. Up ahead the path narrowed into a dark copse of willow. She looked back and could no longer see the parking lot or the bridge spanning the river. Then she remembered what her aunts had said, how, finished with their stories about cockfights, they cast their gaze in this direction and were quiet, if only for a moment, before they told the story.

The boy must have thought she was crazy. Without a

word, she turned and walked in the opposite direction, as if somehow she could get back to the parking lot without him noticing. There, in view of the bridge and the well-traveled road that led to it, they talked, never mentioned her abrupt about-face. They skirted talk of fear or dashed hope. He was a gentleman, she said, this handsome white boy with a mess of close-cropped blond curls and powder-blue eyes. His small mouth widened unbelievably, unnaturally even, into a broad white smile, which he wasn't doing so much now.

"I didn't know what to tell him," Eileen told me, "how to describe what I saw."

She paused, shrugged her shoulders. She asked if I wanted more lemonade. Already, at ten in the morning, the temperature outside was ninety degrees. The kitchen where we sat was stifling, even with the windows pushed open. The apartment was on the second floor, which didn't help matters, and above a corner deli: I smelled onions and fried meat. Every now and then, our conversation was punctuated by the ring of an old-fashioned cash register.

"What do you mean?" I asked.

"The whole story."

"What story?"

Then she said what she saw.

A woman on the path. Coming with the man wearing the straw sombrero. Her hair, which was fixed for Sunday Mass at St. Rose Church, though jet black, resembles Rita Hayworth's flowing red mane in *Gilda*. She wears a plain skirt and blouse set off by a wide patent leather belt and matching shoes. Her stomach swells slightly below the belt; she's not pregnant, thank God; today or tomorrow she will menstruate. Thank God, because she has six children, hard enough already.

She was both surprised and thankful that the man wearing the sombrero showed up at her door last night. Surprised because she had wronged him, exercised poor judgment with a coworker in the hop fields, poor judgment he was made privy to; thankful because how many men would be willing to care for a woman with six kids, and then give the woman a second chance.

That was what he had said in the dim porch light: a second chance. He'd come directly to her house after twelve hours mending apple crates in Sebastopol. Their lovemaking was rigorous. In the morning they went to church. He had only his work clothes, but she had ironed them. He showered and used her oldest boy's aftershave. He left his hat on the pew when they took Communion. After, he wanted to go for a ride, just the two of them, the kids could take care of themselves.

She knew a place.

She had picked mountain balm with her grandmother and great-aunts there. She remembered summer days, and the sharp scent of the herb, but, most of all, the appeal of the slow-moving green water. She knew about the cockfights— what Indian woman hereabouts didn't?—which was how she knew where to direct him off the road to park.

Just north, upriver from where they left the car, there was a wide, empty circle of tramped earth. A column of fennel, like a gatepost, grew alongside the trail. Chicken feathers specked the ground and clung to clumps of chaparral that loosely enclosed the circle—gold and red and black feathers, like left-over decorations. A faint line of smoke wafted from a heap of ashes. The still emptiness of the scene, felt in the noon-day light, emboldened her. Crossing the circle, she felt alive, complete, as if she had been present at the cockfight the night before and she alone had survived its chaos. She was not carry-ing another man's baby. They could start over, a clean slate, she and the man wearing the straw sombrero.

They pass the orange flowers and taller, sticky-leafed plants; no doubt, the man is leading now, because he sees, up ahead, where it is they are going. She isn't paying attention. Maybe she's glancing down at her shoes, seeing how dust has filled the cracks in her patent leather: miniscule etchings, like rivers drawn on a map. And then, all at once, in the blink of an eye, they are in the willows, the woman and the man, and she is looking back to the light.

Did she feel a chill in the shadows and remember again her grandmother and the herbs, not the sun and warm days but wintertime, when she had a cold, felt a tightening in her chest, and the old woman was taking the dried leaves from a Mason jar to boil tea? Or maybe she was just looking back up the trail, if only for a way back to the light? Or maybe she didn't have time, even to comprehend what he was saying, that no other man would have her, for it happened so fast, one of his arms securing her head, the other forcing the hot blade into her swelled abdomen again and again.

Eileen knew details. But how? Had her aunts read the man's confession in a newspaper? Did they see a photo of him? Or had an ordinary and horrible story grown legs and feet?

"I didn't really see her until I was back at the car," Eileen said. "It was just this thing that came over me . . . Stupid, I guess. That boy was cute. He must've thought I was an idiot. We kept talking. How could I tell him I was seeing that woman looking back at me?"

"Maybe she thought of her moon," I suggested.

I figured she wouldn't engage with, at least not favorably,

the moon idea—that the tragic woman, in her last moments, thought of the menstrual taboo that says that not only during her menstruation but also immediately before and after, a woman mustn't hike in the brush, particularly near a body of water, such as a river—but I wanted to impress Eileen with my knowledge of such things. Eileen was proudly Catholic; though aware of Indian traditions, she mostly scoffed at them as backward.

Almost ten years had passed since we'd met in junior high, when neither of us knew we were cousins, descendants of Tom Smith. I'd moved to Los Angeles a year and a half earlier and was home in Santa Rosa visiting. She had acquired her apartment recently and wanted me to see it.

My mind kept whirling with the story she told, imagining the woman's state of mind, the significance of the gruesome tale—and Eileen's experience too, what it meant for her at the time as a sixteen-year-old. She didn't preoccupy herself with so-called Indian lore then either, but hadn't certain notions crossed her mind? Even now, seven years later, wasn't she repressing thoughts of taboo?

As if she were reading my mind, she answered dryly, "What difference does it make, a woman got murdered, isn't that enough?"

I was gazing out her window, to the rooftops across the street. I looked back to her, if only not to be rude.

The first time I had been to Wohler Bridge, passing over it, was with Mabel McKay, who taught me about everything worthwhile I know. Again, it was summertime, the year before I moved to Los Angeles. In those days, I often drove Mabel to pick herbs or dig sedge for basket making. If I remember correctly, we were on our way to Dry Creek to explore the sedge beds (now below Warm Springs Dam's three hundred feet of water).

As always, she was noting features of the landscape. She nodded upriver and said that she had heard of a good place to pick mountain balm there. Was it her longtime friend Essie Parrish who had told her of the place? We were somewhere in border territory, historically shared by Coast Miwok, Kashaya Pomo, and Southern Pomo—obviously not in Mabel's native Cache Creek Pomo region of eastern Lake County. What I remember is her mentioning how, at that time of year, the mountain balm, indeed many herbs, would be mature; "mature time" was how she put it, and I was struck, finding not only her use of the word but her tone more suitable to a group of well-behaved schoolchildren, or perhaps an elder, say a woman after menopause.

When I visited Eileen, I was on my way to Wohler Bridge, or on my way back, I should say, for a second visit. On a tip from a friend, I'd learned of the place as a haven for nude sunbathing. It was 1974. I was twenty-two years old. I didn't tell her that I had been to the place, or that I was on my way back, only that I'd heard that young people were hanging out there, nude sunbathing, which was what prompted her stories about the area. We had gone our separate ways, her to a job, me to college, and I wasn't certain how she felt about the idea of public nudity and didn't want to offend her sense of propriety.

That seems so long ago. Recently, Eileen let me know, with an ironic chuckle, that she was aware of my visits to Wohler Bridge. A mutual friend had described my presence there, Eileen said, "in a flattering manner." Now I was the one embarrassed, a middle-aged man face-to-face with a middle-aged female cousin and childhood friend. Today we know our connection to Tom Smith, how exactly we are cousins. And I know many stories that connect me to the place in specific ways, including that Tom Smith and other Coast Miwok ancestors followed the Russian River inland from the coast to pick herbs there (long before the appearance of a bridge)— mountain balm as well as angelica, which once grew in abundance in a damp recess nearby—and that, many years later, my

Filipino grandfather, with my Coast Miwok grandmother (Tom Smith's granddaughter) on his arm, watched the notorious cockfights, saw feathers fly there.

I have returned to Wohler Bridge several times. I've watched the crowds dwindle, particularly as the door closed on the now unbelievable era between the pill and AIDS, and then altogether disappear when the property owner, reputed to have been the late actor Fred MacMurray, fenced off all access and posted very noticeable No Trespassing signs. Older now, I am nostalgic for those days of bliss in the sun. I went there to relax, escape worries of school and whatever else, to forget.

Thirty-five years since my first visit, I returned once more. Driving along Eastside Road, across the bridge, adjacent the stand of redwoods, I discovered a parking lot and then, past an open chain-link gate, a trail leading back to the river. An Asian couple stood fishing on the shore, dungarees rolled up to their knees, crude bamboo poles extended over the green water. Farther upriver, parked against a massive redwood trunk, one man, and then, not far away, another, both clad in flannel shirts on this hot day, stared out at the river and beach across. Were they waiting for fun reminiscent of the old days, or just remembering it?

I forged the river, swam across. Still a beach; no people on this side but still a beach, sand, the water. And of course that eternal summer light. I plopped down, felt the beach sand, cool water dripping down my shoulders.

The osprey, that magnificent bird that burst from the empty sky, broke my bliss. I watch now as it follows the river and vanishes as effortlessly as it appeared. I've seen ospreys here before. Like this one, they always seem to come from nowhere. A knowledgeable fellow sunbather from days gone by speculated that ospreys had a nest in the redwoods across the water. She said they had great vision, able to see far distances and into the water many, many feet—their eyes shielded from the sun's reflection on the water's surface. They can live thirty years or more. Had I seen this same bird before? Was it now searching the water for a plump carp?

Still, even in the osprey's absence, the place stirs; the world is set in motion again and the hours march slowly on. The faintest trace of shadow. The monkey plant and the mountain balm, leaning, anticipate the afternoon. My mind is wild with stories.

I think of them all: Eileen and the farm boy with the blond curls; the woman with Rita Hayworth hair and the man wearing the straw sombrero; my grandfather and grandmother and the swirling dust of fighting roosters; old man Tom Smith, one leg slightly bowed, picking mountain balm leaves. Then, just as fast, I remember Mabel, not when we drove over the bridge, when she said "mature," but her warning me—I hear her actually—saying not to tell stories after and before the frost, after and before winter season, not only because you must pay attention to where you are going, watchful for snakes and such, but because you too are coming out, becoming story. It was the rule, she said, and added, for my benefit it seemed, that it was silly to think of stories all the time.

But the stories won't let up. They converge in a moment. My own story, I think—what happened when I came back here after visiting Eileen.

I see it.

Coming along the dusty path, the orange flowers and sticky leaves coming into view, even the copse of willow up ahead, and I'm thinking of the stories I have just heard from Eileen. But, no matter, because I don't follow the path but turn to the beach instead.

There are lots of people: unclad bathers lining the sand.

It is a glorious day, and I am glorious in it. I am twenty-two. Earlier, before my stop at Eileen's apartment, I had paid a visit to the gym, and I still feel pumped up. My seventies stylishly-long hair, mustache . . . I wasn't thinking about stories, and yet this is the same story again. No, not the set of eyes I felt upon me when I turned and glimpsed, beside a cottonwood, a spectacular form clad only in a string of beads (I told myself to compliment the beads, talk about the damn multicolor beads), and not even the line drawn in the sand by the shade. The story happened when I stopped, before a single thought entered my head. It was then, for however long that moment was, that I was more alive and smart in this place, indeed in the whole world, than ever before.

This is summer, I was thinking. Knowing summer for the first time.

Then my reverie is broken by the sound of a truck approaching on a dirt road behind me, and I remember that I am trespassing. I dive into the water, heading for the other side.

SCAR

Fall.

Mrs. Ianucci, the babysitter, had a scar that, as I remember it, resembled in shape and dimension the continent of South America. She had stepped into her backyard, no doubt hearing dogs bark, to see what was going on, and had thought in her haste only to button the top button of her sleeveless blouse, and there it was, emblazoned like a tattoo atop her hard, protruding stomach, the purple scar. Behind her the canopy of a weeping willow fell like a curtain. It was morning. In the bright light she looked as if she were on a stage, alone and there for me to see.

"None of the chickens are out, are they?" she asked, unself-consciously scratching the side of her face.

Where my parents found Mrs. Ianucci I have no idea, perhaps through friends, since in those days friends often shared babysitters. We'd had a run of babysitters: Mrs. Hycee, an elderly woman, permed white hair and cardigan sweater, who nursed a glass of beer while working her crossword puzzle on the kitchen table; Myra, divorced, pale and pockmarked, who sat in the same chair as Mrs. Hycee, head bent over an open real estate manual, preparing for her exam; and various teenage girls, too young or too plain to have dates, who started homework on the kitchen table but ended up in front of the TV, eyes fixed on an episode of *Gunsmoke* or *The Twilight Zone*.

Mrs. Ianucci was my parents' age, mid-thirties or so, a mother herself with two sons, both older than me. She was short, thick arms and legs. Her clothes, though clean, often looked mismatched, as if put together hastily without much thought. There was nothing unusual or remarkable about her general appearance except that when she wore lipstick, which wasn't all the time, the lipstick was so bright and thick on her lips that as a nine-year-old I couldn't help staring. Then I saw her eyes, watery blue orbs, wide and disturbed. I felt self-conscious, quietly looked away, not so much because I was caught staring but because Mrs. Ianucci's eyes betrayed something unsettling, frightening even, about Mrs. Ianucci, and I had seen as much.

She came into our house, leather purse over her shoulder, and my parents, hurrying out the door, probably never noticed her eyes. Neither did my sister and brothers. She sat alone with me at the kitchen table, telling stories about unusual people she knew. Sometimes she did card tricks, pulling a deck from her purse, then shuffling the cards this way and that between her chunky fingers. But mostly she talked: about someone named Alice, who had different-colored eyes and, at forty, was training to be a sword swallower for the circus; about someone else named Gloria, who had hair to her knees and, depressed, hadn't come out of her house for ten years; about someone named Salvatore, an old Italian, a neighbor of hers, who lived in a shack with no electricity or running water. I was rapt with her stories. Our time together was exciting, but also it felt clandestine, as if my being alone with Mrs. Ianucci and listening to her stories was something illicit. Which was probably why I never mentioned a word about it to my parents.

When my sister complained that Mrs. Ianucci only paid attention to me, I worried she might reveal to my parents my secret. "Yeah," I said, "and if it wasn't for me and Mrs. Ianucci talking, you wouldn't get to stay up so late."

Shortly before the last time Mrs. Ianucci babysat us, she pulled from her leather purse a set of tarot cards. Earlier, while she stood behind my mother, fastening a string of pearls at the back of my mother's neck—my father, waiting for my mother in the car, had honked half a dozen times already—I overheard Mrs. Ianucci say, "Mary, I learned how to read cards and it really works. Maybe the cards can help you." My mother looked at me and rolled her eyes.

Mrs. Ianucci laid out the cards and read her friends' fortunes: Alice would soon face misfortune but in the end be all the wiser for it; Gloria would soon get past her slump; and Salvatore, the old Italian, he was going to come into a fortune, though in Mrs. Ianucci's estimation, independent of anything discerned from the cards, he wouldn't change his living conditions one iota. "What about me?" I asked.

Mrs. Ianucci didn't lay out the cards for me. I realized then, with my question still floating somewhere between us, that not only had I never asked her for anything but, for as long as we'd been having these private meetings—several months, nearly as long as she'd been babysitting us—I'd uttered hardly a word at the table. I was confused and disappointed when she wouldn't read my cards, and moreso when she said, "You talk too much."

Now, nearly fifty years later, I find myself seated on a cement bench outside the Coddingtown shopping mall, facing northwest toward Mrs. Ianucci's house. So much has changed.

For instance, here, where the mall and its crowded parking lots sit, I remember prune orchards, rows and rows of trees, and about a mile northwest, where there are strip malls and industrial buildings, warehouses and such, I remember open fields and farmhouses, Mrs. Ianucci's small house among them.

It is seven o'clock in the evening, late September, the autumn light is rich, golden and ocher. My cousin Eileen, seated with me on the bench, pulls onto her lap the red plastic bag containing the CDs I bought her.

"Those prunes," she says, "picking those goddamned prunes. Do you remember how the yellow jackets would get on them?"

Eileen likes to reminisce. We've been sitting on the bench ten minutes and she has recalled several memories: the boys' dean in junior high whom she described as "porky-faced"; the time when, as teenagers, we'd coerced a homeless man to buy beer for us; the fate of two cousins; and now prune-picking. She'd started with the memories at dinner, while we were in line at a Chinese smorgasbord, and, forty-five minutes later in the music store, she was still going.

After thirty years away, I had moved home to Santa Rosa. If it wasn't for the fact that Eileen was mostly calling up a past I remembered, you'd have thought she was already trying to catch me up on everything I had missed. The last time I'd seen her was after my mother died. I'd gone to the funeral home before the rosary to sit with the coffin and collect my thoughts. Thinking I had been alone, I was surprised when I turned and found Eileen, several pews behind me, kneeling, head bowed.

She keeps on about the prunes—how, if she wanted new school clothes in the fall, she had to pick prunes, and the only good thing about picking prunes was that schools didn't open until after the harvest. She had mentioned my mother earlier —that my mother worked in the mall—and maybe that is why I'm thinking of Mrs. Ianucci now. Or is it because I'm facing in the direction of where Mrs. Ianucci once lived? Yet, it's not memories of my mother behind the men's furnishings counter at JCPenney that comes to mind, nor Mrs. Ianucci's house or her babysitting, or even her storytelling, but her scar. It's there, grotesque, plain to see in that morning light, whenever I think of Mrs. Ianucci.

If my mother never said where she found Mrs. Ianucci, neither did she say at the time why she disappeared. We already hadn't seen Mrs. Ianucci for about six months when my parents got divorced. Looking back, it was as if the house was suddenly tilted on end and my frantic mother was running helter-skelter attempting to keep everything from sliding away. She couldn't hold on to my pets: two jersey heifers and a flock of bantam chickens. The heifers went to a dairy. The chickens went to Mrs. Ianucci, I suppose because my mother could think of no one else to keep them, and although she was never particularly enthused about driving me to and from Mrs. Ianucci's house to visit the chickens, no doubt she couldn't think of another way to compensate me for the loss. They were pairs of Mille Fleurs, speckled like pheasants, and Cochins with feathered legs and feet.

Roaming dogs had recently killed one hen, and Mrs. Ianucci had been keeping all the rest locked up. When she came out with her scar showing, I simply told her none of the chickens was out, expecting her to go right back inside. But she didn't move. I'm certain she saw me staring. After a moment, she said something about a horse her youngest son had bought, but I was barely listening. I kept waiting for her to button her blouse, but she never did, not even when she turned finally and went back into the house.

"What about Mrs. Ianucci?" I say to Eileen.

"Remember when we snuck up on Mrs. Ianucci and that old wino?" she rejoins, and I see in my mind's eye what she tells next.

That old wino was Salvatore, the Italian, Mrs. Ianucci's neighbor, who lived in a shack with no electricity or running water.

Eileen, with her mother and sisters, had moved from town to a house on Hardies Lane, Mrs. Ianucci's street. The house was unpainted. Weeds grew up along the fence, tall as the roses. Like much of the property in the area, the house had been sold months before to developers. I was fifteen or thereabouts, and I had not seen Mrs. Ianucci for four years at least. Four years is a long time in a kid's life. I'd learned to let go of my two heifers and the chickens—I didn't have much choice, since my mother had taken a job and had no time to drive me to visit them anymore—and until Eileen gave me directions to her new house on Hardies Lane, I hadn't thought of Mrs. Ianucci either.

"I knew this lady who lived up the street—Mrs. Ianucci," I said.

Eileen and I were seated on the couch. Eileen's mother stood in the doorway between the front room and kitchen. Eileen was short and dark, attractive beyond her years, jet black hair and eyes, an Indian for sure. Her mother, on the other hand, was light-skinned and tall, with a mass of red hair that, until I had mentioned Mrs. Ianucci, she was busy plucking pink and purple foam curlers from. Now she stood looking at me.

"She's a crazy woman," she said. "How the hell do you know her?"

Eileen's mother was defiant, certainly not one to mince words. Though just then, with her face lit by the evening sun pouring through a window, she looked weary. She dropped a curler into the glass bowl atop a stack of unpacked boxes.

"My mother used to know her," I said.

A self-conscious teenager, late to mature, unlike Eileen, I didn't want to call up the fact that I had ever needed a baby-sitter. Or was it that, remembering Mrs. Ianucci's storytelling at my kitchen table, I accepted Eileen's mother's assessment as true and didn't want to be associated with her?

An hour later, after a horn honked and Eileen's mother disappeared, Eileen told me what her mother meant by crazy. Mrs. Ianucci sometimes paraded up and down her driveway in a black bathing suit and high heels; occasional loud shrieks from her house woke neighbors in the middle of the night; and, according to some of those same neighbors, on weekends, when Mrs. Ianucci's husband worked the late shift at the shoe factory, she visited the old Italian, who, far from being poor, had wads of money hidden under his shack, which he used to pay Mrs. Ianucci for sex.

"Maybe she visits him because she wants someone to speak Italian with," I offered.

Eileen laughed. She said that it was Mr. Ianucci who was Italian, that Mrs. Ianucci was neither Italian nor spoke Italian. I wondered how she knew this when I, who actually knew Mrs. Ianucci, didn't. More importantly, I saw my cue.

"Let's go see . . . It's the weekend. Look at the clock."

I was surprised Mrs. Ianucci was still around, much less in the same house. Again, four years is an eternity in a kid's life. Hadn't she faded away somewhere?

My curiosity was aroused. What had happened to my chickens? Had Mrs. Ianucci gotten worse? If Eileen's mother was correct, that Mrs. Ianucci was crazy, then was everything I had experienced with her, all those bizarre stories, an early symptom of her madness? Had my parents seen as much and fired her—perhaps the business with her tarot cards? Now I had an opportunity to catch a glimpse of her.

Eileen was reluctant. Cast as babysitter with her mother's disappearance, she was responsible for her four younger sisters, plus her mother had asked her to finish unpacking boxes. Ultimately, I persuaded her to come with, saying we would simply sneak a peek and come right back. She shot me a glance that suggested I was out of my mind.

There *was* an old man named Salvatore, or at least an old man, Italian or not, who lived two short fields from Mrs. Ianucci, which I knew because once, while I was visiting my chickens, Mrs. Ianucci pointed over her barbed wire fence to a shack, more like a squat barn, and I spied a skulking figure in overalls moving about the place. I looked for signs of electricity—a TV antenna, wires extending from the telephone pole on the street—and found none. Wasn't he old then? How old would he be now? Sex with Mrs. Ianucci? It seemed incredible to me, but I figured I might get to see Mrs. Ianucci nonetheless. Eileen and I could steal into her yard and peer through her windows. But then, only halfway out of Eileen's yard, we stopped suddenly. Mrs. Ianucci was passing on the street. It was dark, and we couldn't see her well, only her white dress billowing in the breeze as she made her way away from us.

We waited some time on Eileen's porch step. Of course Mrs. Ianucci could have been going anywhere, maybe just taking a walk. It was a balmy late-summer night, after all. But I didn't suggest as much to Eileen, lest she have more reason not to take the adventure. I said, "Okay, let's go," and Eileen said dryly, "What, you think they're having sex by now?"

The thought of Mrs. Ianucci and an old man having sex

wasn't appealing, certainly. I had thought of her scar, but I didn't expect to see it, not unless we discovered her naked, again not appealing. What was driving me? Seeing Mrs. Ianucci after all this time? Seeing her now a full-fledged crazy woman? Was it just the sheer excitement of possibly seeing something I wasn't supposed to, of getting away with something?

"What else are we going to do, sit in your house all night?" I answered Eileen.

The shack was a square silhouette in the middle of an empty field. A dirt road led to it from the street. We crawled through a wire fence, then crouched as we scuttled across the field. There was nothing to hide behind, not until we came to a low-growing fig tree, but by then we were next to the shack. There was the sharp scent of ripe figs. Through the leafy foliage faint light shone from an open window.

"They'll hear us," Eileen whispered.

Old leaves littered the ground. There didn't seem to be any other windows, not on this side of the shack, and it would have been stupid to risk passing an open door. What if the old man had a dog?

Not a sound came from the window. I poked Eileen with my finger, urging her forward. She grabbed ahold of my finger and with it shoved my hand away. Alone, I edged forward then, gingerly stepping over the leaves toward the window. When I looked back, I couldn't see Eileen. She was on the other side of the tree. I was below the window.

Peering over the ledge, I saw a stovepipe and pots hanging from big nails or bolts on the opposite wall. Rising up, my line of vision taking in more of the room, I saw the old man, gray-whiskered, wizened, in dirty overalls and a stained long-sleeved cotton shirt, then Mrs. Ianucci, below me, just the back of her head, the same unremarkable brown hair drooping in loose curls to her shoulders. One might have thought them an old farmer and his daughter or granddaughter, or maybe an old farmer and his young wife. There was a card table between them and not much else in the sparse room. Besides the cast iron stovetop below the stovepipe, I could see little else. A kerosene lamp burned atop an adjacent counter, which was stacked with some canned goods. An empty plate and a bunched-up napkin were on the table; perhaps he had just finished dinner. She was reading a movie magazine. At one point, he muttered something—in Italian—and I ducked down. But when I looked again, he was gazing blankly, and she was still reading her magazine.

When I heard Eileen heading back across the field, I followed her.

What did I have to report? I saw the old man, and I saw the back of Mrs. Ianucci's head.

She was indeed there, but so what?

"Maybe she fixed him dinner—maybe that's what she does going down there," Eileen said, both of us seated again on her couch.

But there had to be more. Thirty minutes later I went back alone. No way could I coerce Eileen to go a second time, I didn't even try.

I was careful crossing the field and sidling past the fig tree, but I felt more reckless, exposed somehow. Mrs. Ianucci was talking—the voice I remembered—about someone—her sister-in-law?—borrowing something and not giving it back. I never heard what it was she lost, but she was peeved and her husband hadn't stuck up for her. She was still talking when I peeked over the window ledge, but she was busy packing her magazine into her purse on the table, and the old man, mouth agape, was in his chair dead asleep.

Figuring she was getting ready to leave, I tore away while I still had the chance, before she might come out and find me. Past the fig tree, I could still hear the sound of her voice.

I wanted to tell Eileen something fantastic: that Mrs. Ianucci had fallen into a trance and started speaking in tongues. Or something gross: they were having sex.

"I think she was talking to herself," I said, not able to come up with anything else.

The adventure, short of allowing me a peek at Mrs. Ianucci, and even then only the back of her head, provided no insights, no answers. I could not prove or disprove any of Eileen's stories about her—whether or not she was a crazy woman. If I wasn't disappointed then, I am now, as if Eileen's mentioning the escapade should have been more than the mere memory of an uneventful childhood prank. Did I expect somehow to learn something new about Mrs. Ianucci? Did I expect Eileen to explain the scar? I never told her, or anyone, about the scar. Perhaps because I felt embarrassed for having seen it, for having looked in the first place, and for continuing to look, as if Mrs. Ianucci, a woman my mother's age, was naked and I was intrigued with what I was seeing. Still, I want to ask Eileen something about that night—I don't know what—but of course she's on to something else, a story about an argument one of her sisters had at an Indian Health Clinic picnic over how to cook hamburgers.

Ever since I'd moved back to Santa Rosa, I'd been trying to find myself in the place. I was often lost: What was where the Post Office is now? Wasn't there a hill where Yardbirds sits?

My mother, who might have helped me, is gone. It's a wonder I didn't call and ask Eileen to dinner sooner. She never left this town. Over the years, I checked in with her whenever I visited, and our time together was the same, full of reminiscences and current stories. I could connect past to present. In the music store I bought her two of our favorite CDs: Otis Redding's greatest hits, with "Dock of the Bay," and Aretha Franklin's *Gold*, with "Respect." But now she is getting on my nerves. Granted, she usually does most of the talking, but she's incessant, going a mile a minute, like I've never seen her, all of it feeling as meaningless as the memory of an uneventful childhood prank.

I met Eileen in junior high, eighth grade. I had a crush on her. She accommodated me for a while, which surprised me, since, gangly and immature, I considered myself out of her league. No doubt she understood all along that I was better suited for a friend and not a boyfriend. An older guy, truly tough, with bulging biceps and a gold cross chain, whisked her away soon enough. He was her cousin, too. In my defense, I didn't know Eileen and I were related. I didn't even know I was Indian.

I was living in Menlo Park, in grad school at Stanford, when I learned about my father. When I told Eileen the news, she didn't seem surprised or excited. Was it because she'd already had a cousin boyfriend? Or was it that, because Tom Smith had many, many children, there was always a chance any two Indians from Sonoma County might be related? Maybe she didn't believe me: with fair skin, I look white. In any event, she started talking soon about something else.

She lives with one of her sisters in a new apartment building west of town. She was married once, for a short while after high school. Those days, she worked with her mother in the fisheries. She took some business classes and got a job at PG&E, in customer services I think, and after that was a receptionist for a community health program. A while ago, she was in a car accident, serious, and though she seems to have recovered, she hasn't returned to work full-time. She babysits her sister's grandson a few hours after school, and sometimes on the weekends caretakes for an elderly man. Her room in the apartment is small, neat as a pin. She's proud of the ingenious manner with which she has made shelves with wood planks and cinder blocks, sturdy enough to hold a new CD player and speakers on the top shelf. "People think I'm crazy keeping all this stuff, but look," she said, pointing to several plastic crates stacked against a wall. CDs and old record albums, magazines, school yearbooks, family mementos and scrapbooks—the crates were crammed full, yet everything was labeled, and she took pains, lifting heavy crates, to read every file, even as I stood, keys in hand, waiting to go to dinner. Was that when her incessant talking began? It occurs to me that she is drunk, or high on something.

There is so much we could be talking about. Our shared history, for instance. I see our great-great-grandfather, Tom Smith, on a wagon, leather reins in his hands, following a dirt road across this valley. From where he lived, in Bodega Bay, it took sometimes half a day to get to Santa Rosa by wagon. But he had songs, they say hummingbird songs, and he could get here in the blink of an eye. Once, at the edge of town, there was a woman suffocating, asthma or maybe consumption, and he pulled a bird out of her chest. Another time, he made a small incision on the back of a man's head—to extract an insect causing headaches—then tossed the piece of sharp quartz he used into Santa Rosa Creek.

It is fall. Mabel McKay used to say: "It is a prayerful time. Pay attention because you are taking from the earth what you will need to live on during the winter. Be prayerful, be watchful, or you won't have enough." I imagine my ancestors hereabouts in this autumn twilight. Men and women sort through a cache of acorns spilled on the ground. Their faces and the rich designs in the upturned burden baskets flicker in the fire-light. Maybe they think of ancient-time stories, Coyote stories. They won't tell them when it's too dark to work any longer—it is forbidden until after the first frost—but already they antici-pate the long nights ahead.

Eileen talks about hamburgers—hamburgers!—and how the nephew she babysits is a brat, probably has ADD; how her sister, the grandmother of the brat, is diabetic and eats every-thing she shouldn't. And did I know that food additives make people crazy, that canned tuna is full of mercury, and that eventually we're all going to get done in by global warming? Billy, a kid we knew in junior high, has hepatitis C, and Angie Williams, his girlfriend then, still lives with her mother . . .

Eileen has aged since the last time I saw her. It's strange to think both of us are older now than her mother was that night we spied on Mrs. Ianucci. Her hair is dyed red, which made me think of her mother when I first saw her. She keeps herself up well, and it wasn't her hair or the few lines on her face that made me think she looked older but that quality you sometimes see in people who were heavier earlier in their lives and are now thinner—not shrunken or withered, just smaller. She never has been much interested in a history beyond her lived experience. She is a Catholic and is ambivalent at best about Indian traditions. I don't expect profound conversations about Tom Smith, or whatever else that's Indian. It's not that she's not talking about Tom Smith that really bothers me now, but her aimless babbling. It's grating. I wish I could take her home, but she won't stop talking.

The color of the night deepens and I feel more anxious. My mind wanders again. I remember picking prunes, and Eileen and her sisters joking about the old Indian women who sometimes packed prunes in burden baskets—"Can tell they're Indians!"—and I see the old women, traditional long dresses, and on their backs burden baskets, impossibly heavy with purple fruit.

Then I catch the words, Eileen saying, "I knew my mother was dead, but I put it on her just the way she did, the lipstick, the eye shadow, last the hair."

I am struck. I know the story, how the undertaker, for whatever reasons, asked Eileen to make up her mother's face before the funeral. Eileen told me about this years before; in fact, she's told me about it a couple of times, repeating herself, so it's not as if the image it invokes is anything new. But now I can't get the picture out of my mind: Eileen bent over her mother's corpse, cylinder of lipstick between her fingers, etching bright gloss onto her mother's lips, carefully, as if her mother might rise up and correct her.

She's quiet now. Was she talking for my benefit? Was she talking over her own pain? She's not at all drunk or high. She's landed on a memory too painful to continue talking. She's stumbled and so have I, but I understand this only after I understand what is happening. Everything has come together at once. My mother. The town. Eileen and I sitting on a bench outside the mall. Tom Smith. Of course, Mrs. Ianucci. The image tells me everything that matters now. What's Eileen been doing? What's this storytelling, now or in the depths of winter, incessant or not, but a covering of the cold and dark with a semblance of life?

I can understand Mrs. Ianucci, or begin to. And my obsession with her scar. I don't know how she got the scar. An operation? An accident? I don't know either if she is still alive—I think the last time I saw her was the night I spied on her. Certainly she doesn't live on Hardies Lane anymore. But at least I know a story I can tell. About a boy who caught sight of misfortune, a tear in the fabric of life, represented by an ugly scar over a woman's bare stomach. In the same vein, I'd like to imagine that Mrs. Ianucci saw in her tarot cards that I would be a writer, and by telling me that I talked too much, she was advising me to watch the world carefully, to listen. But that is another story.

I'm ashamed of my impatience. But my feet are on the ground. This is fall. Each story that rises from the landscape takes on its purple hue, as far as I can see. The sky, like an upturned basket, reaches to the horizons. At this moment I could turn it upright and carry it off.

PLACES

FIDEL'S PLACE

Three days after the Indian—I'll call him Fidel—avenged the assault on his wife and slayed the young rancher who'd committed the horrible deed, the posse of vigilantes pursuing him found him, not near the small settlement of Marshall but across Tomales Bay on a ridge, and not in a thicket of coyote brush and low-growing fir, where he might've hidden, but in the middle of an open grassland. Seemingly oblivious to the sound of approaching horses, he was standing, taking in the view, continuing to look over his shoulder at the expansive Pacific and then back across the bay to the eastern hills from which he'd come. Even when the men shouted threats, dismounted, and aimed their bayonet-clad rifles at him, he did not waver. He didn't look as if he'd been running for days; his clothes on that fogless morning were clean, and he wore a brightly colored shirt, perhaps white or scarlet, creating the impression, along with his indifference to their approach, that he actually wanted to be found. Surrender.

The men continued to bark orders, bayonets jutting from their rifles only feet from him, and all he did was drop his gaze to the grass where he'd been standing, then look back to the open prairie, his head twisted around, even as they marched him, shackled, down to the boat that would carry him across the water to Marshall.

I was twelve or thereabouts when I first heard about Fidel. A friend's mother, I believe a descendant of Fidel, told the story. Like many Coast Miwok from Tomales Bay, my friend's mother had moved north to Santa Rosa a couple decades before, shortly after World War II, looking for work, and she often reminisced with her sisters about "the old days in Marshall"—sharing stories not just with each other but for any kids who sat at her kitchen table and listened.

I never liked the story. I found it moralizing, admonishing —for while this man Fidel had great powers, including the ability to shape-shift into a hummingbird, which would have allowed him to escape his captors, he could not use them because he had broken the tacitly understood rule that those who possessed these powers should not commit murder. But after decades of dislocation and abuse (this story took place in the late 1860s or early 1870s), to find your wife gagged and tied under the thrall of a white man and not do anything—or to get punished for seeking justice—just didn't seem fair. Hearing the tale, I, probably like others listening in, sublimated the part of the story I didn't like and focused instead on Fidel's revenge, how he survived. "If you go to Marshall on a night when there is no fog," my friend's mother said, "you can sometimes see on that treeless ridge across the water an enormous green light."

For Coast Miwok people, like all indigenous peoples of central California, the landscape was nothing less than a richly layered text, a sacred book; each ocean cove, even the smallest seemingly unassuming rock or tract of open grassland—each feature of the natural world was a mnemonic peg on which individuals could see a story connected to other stories and thus know and find themselves home. Villages, indeed entire nations, were not only associated with particular locales but actually named after them. Hence, the tribal nation that occupied most of the territory encompassing what is now called Point Reyes National Seashore called itself Olema, Coyote's Home. A large village overlooking Drakes Bay was Pusuluma, Olivella Shell Ridge; and the open grassland ridge and shoreline just north of Lairds Landing on Tomales Bay, where vigilantes found Fidel on that fogless summer morning, was called Calupetamal, Hummingbird Coast.

By the late 1860s or early 1870s, the landscape of the region had been greatly transformed, much of the homescape trampled, unreadable. The fir forests were logged, the waterways dammed or dredged, the herds of elk and pronghorn all but gone. Overgrazing and foreign seed in the dung of the cattle and horses combined to unsettle the prairie grasslands, replacing the deep-rooted perennial bunchgrasses and sedges with exotic annuals like European oatgrass. European settlement thus spelled dis-settlement; and for the Natives the dis-settlement was both personal and historical, psychological and environmental.

Members of the Olema nation, and of Guaulen, just south of the Olema, were among the first Coast Miwok to be taken into the missions, specifically into Mission Dolores in San Francisco, as early as 1818. Many survivors of the missions and the subsequent Mexican rancho period ended up on a tract of land near present-day Nicasio. When these survivors were booted out of Nicasio by Americans in the early 1860s, many went west to Tomales Bay and settled along the shore. Today, however, no known Coast Miwok trace their ancestry back to an Olema village; most of the mission survivors originated from eastern locales, and many were the descendants of intermarriage between Spanish or Mexican settlers. Yet stories of the place persisted; perhaps some Olema survivors had returned to—or even led others to—the region. In the old tradition, the survivors rooted themselves to the place and began to call themselves Tomales Bay Indians.

I saw the green light. On one of those many trips from Santa Rosa to Marshall in the middle of the night, a dozen of us packed into a car or onto a truck bed, didn't I see the ball of green light atop the ridge across the water? "I see it," someone always said. Maybe I didn't see it and only know it in my imagination. The shape of the grassland ridge that rises above the bay was there, visible even in the dark night.

And it is there today, the open prairie of Tomales Point, bordered by brush and sparse live oak, not unlike the prairie grasslands elsewhere along the seashore. I've made several trips to this place in recent years, stood in the grass and taken in the views. Tule elk have been reintroduced, but where they once roamed freely, now they are contained by fences maintained for the local dairy ranchers: more black-and-white Holsteins dot the peninsula's grassland than elk. Yet always the man Fidel rises up from the grass, visible before me, bright shirt, his demeanor resolved, and I am set to wonder about him, though now it's not the green light or the drama of his last days that intrigues me but the question regarding this place—why he stopped in the open, as if his only reason for fleeing the law was to come to this particular spot.

The grasslands were always a safe haven, not only for herds of elk and pronghorn to graze, and for us to hunt, but also as refuge from the grizzlies less visible in the forests, behind brush. Villages were always located adjacent to grasslands, and in fact, controlled burning of the grasslands kept the brush and encroaching trees in check. After European settlement, when Natives were forbidden to burn, much of the grassland was taken over by coyote brush and Douglas fir.

Fidel, though, wasn't hiding. What safety, then, in the open space? He could've run south from Marshall, not turned northward below the bay, and run out onto the narrowing peninsula between ocean and bay, where he would be trapped eventually. Did he simply want to go where he had views? Was there something in the place concerning his totem hummingbird that he had to reconcile before his death? Or was it a memory, certainly of his wife, the strength and delicacy of her fingers as she held a basket and a seed beater while collecting seed for pinole, and, as she went along there, how the hem of her dress caught and lifted atop the grass stalk?

Then Fidel is laughing at me. For, once again, frustrated by my pondering, I follow him across the water to the hanging noose, to the scaffold on which he stands, the mob below, jeering American settlers, somber Indians in the distance, and at last I understand something. It is the grassland itself, the safety it gives in memory. There is the space, yes, on which memory paints its lore. But it is in the grass too—perennials, annuals, roots—grasses that reveal the shape of the land from time immemorial, and continue to rise up there again and again. The prairie, so empty, so full. Is that what Fidel sought—that understanding in the grass?

He is gone, the scaffold empty; and there on that grassland ridge, a light in the brain, he stands, laughing. "What more?" he says. "You told the story."

BLUEBELLY

His name was Mr. Cortese, and with the way he peeked around the corner of the old barn when we went to see him, only his small dark face visible, his very long fingers clasped to the sideboards, he made us think of a lizard, or at least he made me think of a lizard, and now, many years later, I am there once more, seeing him for the first time. I am fourteen. I am holding the four-month-old fawn-colored goat that Mr. Cortese will kill. "There he is," one of the two brothers I have come with says. By this time, the man is coming toward us, and I can see that he is old and small, crouched it seems in his worn T-shirt and dirt-stiff jeans. His hands are huge, and already I imagine the butcher knife clenched in one hand, the wether's soft neck secured with the other. I don't want to watch—I didn't want to accompany Heralio and Isidro to this place where their father sent them with the goat he'd bought for tomorrow's Easter dinner. No, I didn't want to see a butchering, but here I am braving myself through it because, after all, I am supposed to be brave. And then it's over; the two brothers are packing the newspaper-wrapped carcass back to the truck, and, somehow, I am following the old man past the barn to the far end of his property, where there is a crumbling rock wall. "Help me get the ducks back to the barn," he commands over his shoulder.

At the rock wall, he stops. Dozens of bluebelly lizards are perched on the rocks watching us. The sun is shining brightly. It's warm, all at once it seems, as if spring in that instant had jumped over the rock wall and spread itself across the land. The old man points to a small lizard that scurries into a crevice. "I don't want the ducks to scare them," he says. "Sometimes they will try to eat the small ones." He glances down at a couple of large white ducks a few feet from us. I keep looking at the lizards, amazed: dozens of sets of eyes glinting in the sun. "Help me," he says, and we herd the ducks back to the barn.

Now, with rich late-autumn light over the gravel walkway outside my window, and upon the rock wall farther on, I see lizards again everywhere, stationed at the edges of the walkway, perched on the rocks. Looking at me forty-some years later? I am an old man, or an older man. And, after thirty years of living elsewhere, I am home again in Sonoma County, where I was born and grew up.

I live now on Sonoma Mountain, a sacred landmark for my Coast Miwok and Southern Pomo ancestors. Not dramatic in shape, without the sharp peak of Mount Tamalpais or Mount Saint Helena, the mountain seems from a distance a mere assemblage of rolling hills rising out of the Santa Rosa plain. Where is "the mountain"?

Yet its sheer size is astonishing, overseeing from its heights San Pablo Bay to the south and Mount Saint Helena to the north. And once you begin to explore the mountain, whether from its eastern side below Glen Ellen or west from Petaluma, you will find unexpected oak and bay laurel groves, redwoods even, and hidden lakes and springs, and—surprise around a bend—a landscape as complex as any in Sonoma County, or, as a Coast Miwok elder once said, "as beautiful as the designs in our baskets." I did not grow up on the mountain but in town, in Santa Rosa. Still, I heard the old folks talk of the mountain then, the place where the beginning stories were first told, when Coyote, along with the help of his nephew Chicken Hawk and several other animals, created the world as we know it today: this mountain; the Santa Rosa plain below, with its winding creeks and swath of meandering lagoon; the coastal hills directly west and, beyond them, the blue sea; and Mount Tamalpais, all the way south, whose peak rises out of the landscape like the pitched roof of a redwood bark house. Quail was the most beautiful woman then—at the time of Creation, when the animals were still people—and you can still see it if you look below her plume and find her black pearl eyes. There is a story from that ancient time that explains how skunk got his stripes, why woodpecker wears a red cap, and why rattlesnake goes nowhere without his rattle. There's a reason warm winds dance with the fog on this mountain, and a reason too why the bay trees sing a lonesome young man's song. The sun is the oldest of us all—even older than Coyote. Bluebelly lizard knows this. No one knows the sun better.

The bluebelly lizard, formally known as the western fence lizard, is a staple of the rural Bay Area's long, hot summers, as common as the dry grassy hillsides and the sharp smell of bay laurel trees. From light gray to black in color, with multiple dark splotches, this lizard is essentially the colors of the earth and rocks it inhabits, except it has a distinctive sky-colored belly, more pronounced in the males. Sentinel-like, the bluebelly perches atop rocks, tree branches, fences, watchful for food—flies, small moths and spiders, fleas—as well as for predators—hawks, snakes, and larger species of lizards.

The territorial males, known for their push-ups, will, during the mating season from late May through July, stage fierce wrestling matches during which one may lose his tail. But the bluebelly lizard, after losing its tail, will grow another. Perhaps the bluebelly's most distinctive feature for anyone living in or close to Bay Area rural landscapes is its ability to stem the spread of Lyme disease. According to countless studies, ticks that feed on its blood are much less likely to carry the disease.

My ancestors always knew the bluebelly was important. He knows the sun better than any of us, after all. According to the old stories, the sun gave bluebelly a piece of its home—the sky—to wear as a sign of kinship. Sun said to Bluebelly, "With my home on your stomach, the people will always know to remember me. When they see you each spring, again sitting atop the rocks, they will know too that I have returned. Your belly will match the sky where once again I'm looking down." That's why he's one of the first creatures in the spring, and why he sits where the sun can see him.

The bluebelly figures prominently in Native California lore. According to a story told among the Sierra Miwok of the western Sierra foothills, when Coyote made people, Lizard was the one who persuaded Coyote to give humans hands like Lizard's so we could use tools. Among the Chumash of coastal

Southern California, the bluebelly lizard was a person of great importance. There, in the Sierra foothills and along the Southern California coast, Bluebelly is no doubt an important character in the warp and woof of the storied landscapes.

But I don't know those landscapes.

Home is Sonoma County.

Santa Rosa was, forty years ago, still a relatively small town surrounded by agriculture—apple and prune orchards, dairies and chicken farms. Post–World War II sprawl had not yet claimed all the pastures and orchards from the town's edges. I remember once coming upon an abandoned dairy farm and seeing a developer's red flags crisscrossing the empty fields. The milking barn lay in ruins, a pile of heaped cinder blocks, as if the farmer, out of spite over the new zoning ordinance that forced him from his land, had blown up the building. There in the rubble were countless bluebelly lizards, vigilant, watchful, but trusting, it seemed, that nothing—no hawk or snake, no imminent bulldozer—would destroy their kingdom.

One of the first things that appealed to me about my new home on Sonoma Mountain was its numerous rock walls. I moved into the house on a July day, when the mountain was warm, dry. There were plenty of lizards; the rock walls are a perfect habitat for bluebellies. But I didn't think much about them. There was the frenzy of moving, the unloading of boxes, a water pump to repair, a broken window to replace. And then I experienced something I hadn't counted on: anxiety. Could I find my way here after having been gone for so long? Could I settle in? What of the mountain's silence after my years of living in L.A.? Was there a door I could pass through and find myself home again, or might I find myself forever wandering in the dark, dissolved by the silence?

More and more my life on the mountain felt like a vacation that was lasting too long. Yes, I grew up in Sonoma County, but in town, never so far from neighbors; my home now is near the top of the mountain, at the end of a steep and winding dirt road. Not far from my property line, a large Coast Miwok community once thrived. But now? What of those old stories I'd heard as a kid? The chasm between then and now felt impossible to cross. Was there ever a home here? Maybe I should have picked a house in town, I told myself. But, alas, even the town has changed, become unrecognizable: a huge mall where the movie theatres had been; the open fields and orchards I'd remembered now buried under housing tracts and strip malls advertising submarine sandwiches and all-year tans.

Then the land itself came out, pushed open the door I'd been looking for, and poured through. Or, say, Coyote, as tricky and surprising as the mountain he created, came out. It was like this: I am driving home, up the mountain, with a bag of groceries alongside me in the front seat, and I spot a coyote as he trots past a fence post and disappears into the brush. Probably looking for a rabbit, I think. Maybe going back to its den someplace. Isn't that what coyotes do, hunt and live in hollowed tree trunks? And then there's a tickling sensation in my brain, and I'm laughing, laughing at my foolishness. Coyote hunt? Coyote live in a den? What was I thinking? Where had I been? No; Coyote created the world up on the mountain, along with his nephew Chicken Hawk; and, after he was disrespectful to his wife Frog Woman, she left him, living forever after in a lake, which is why to this day he howls at the moon. Quail, she doesn't just lay eggs in my lavender, she has the secret that the lonesome young man from the bay laurel grove needed to seduce the woman he loved. And this lizard, the bluebelly on my rock wall, who else is he but the best friend of the sun? What's before me but trails of stories, one story leading to another, my known home, up the mountain and down. In town, on the Santa Rosa plain, voices rise, up from below a cul-de-sac or a McDonald's: one is from a heavyset Pomo medicine man in suspenders and a top hat who walks with the grace of a hummingbird; another from a girl with a gold tooth who eats a raw egg to exorcise a demon; another an old man with a butcher's knife and a million lizards.

I had presumed Mr. Cortese was Mexican. "No, he's Portuguese or something," said Heralio and Isidro, who were Mexican. Someone else said the old man was Indian, not Coast Miwok or Pomo but Yurok or Hupa, from Humboldt County.

After my visit with Heralio and Isidro, I went again, one more time. The house was small, the yard littered with box springs and rusted car parts. Mr. Cortese raised goats and sheep and ducks, which he traded for staples—rice, flour, a crate of apples. I didn't understand then that, like many recently displaced farmers, he no doubt rented his small farm for a pittance from a developer waiting to build houses on the land. His ducks were Muscovies, big white ducks with fleshy red faces, known to raise large batches of ducklings that grow fast. A cousin wanted to start raising Muscovies. "Feed them well. Do good to them. They'll give lots of babies," Mr. Cortese said after placing a wooden crate containing ducks on the bed of my cousin's pickup.

"I'll help you get the ducks back to the barn," I offered.

I looked to the edge of Mr. Cortese's property, to the rock wall, but no ducks were there, and suddenly I felt stupid.

"Ain't no little lizards now. No lizards at all. Not until summer again." To make his point, he stomped his thick leather boot on the rain-soaked ground.

Looking out my window, beyond the rock wall with its sentinel bluebellies here and there, I see the curled dry leaves of a large oak scattered on the ground below the tree, and falling, one at a time it seems. Behind my house, clumps of poison sumac have turned red. The old bay laurels drop their fruit—peppernuts my ancestors harvested for eons, along with acorns from the oaks. The birds are full-feathered. The deer's coats are long. In two weeks a first frost will cover the land, visible on the summer-dry grass and thistle. Then rain. Short days. Lizards hibernate. No more atop the rocks walls. Not one.

Mabel McKay warned that we should only tell stories during the winter months, after the first frost and before the last. "You must pay attention in summer to where you are going," she said. "Don't be thinking about the stories then."

In the old days people had to pay attention to the land in the summer, lest they step on a rattlesnake or scorpion. And they didn't need stories in summer; they could see where they were going, find their way in a world renewed by the sun. The winter nights, with hours of idle time, certainly provided the opportunity for storytelling, but wasn't it the long hours of darkness that prompted the need? Wouldn't one recall a washed-out hillside after a storm and worry about the changes to the landscape? Would the hill be recognizable? What of seeing the entire Santa Rosa plain under water? What of a memory in that long darkness of a broken path, far from the home village? Wouldn't one then welcome the stories, sing for the animals to chart again a known world?

I've been home five years, settled in. In the waning light outside my window, I see the cusp of winter. I know the long winter nights; I've known too the broken path. Winter? Darkness? Bluebelly, that fellow on my rock wall, hibernate? No. What I know, following him, now and again, is that there will be sun, that there will be a thousand more stories, some told with the pencil in my old man's hand, stories about Coyote and Frog Woman, stories about a medicine man who walks with the grace of a hummingbird, a gold-toothed girl who casts a demon from her body, and an old man with ducks and endless lizards, stories and more stories, until the sun returns to the mountain again and there are new leaves on the trees, I know, quail in the lavender and bluebelly lizards on my rock wall.

THE CHARMS
OF TOLAY LAKE
REGIONAL PARK

A relative told me that when she saw Tom Smith's charmstone, she was temporarily blinded and felt instantly faint—its power was that overwhelming. The charmstone, a smoothly carved rock figure, about an inch and a half in length, was loosed from Tom Smith's "doctoring kit," which had been stored in a drawer at UC Berkeley's Lowie Museum (now the Phoebe Apperson Hearst Museum of Anthropology) for decades following his death in 1934. Grandpa Tom, as he is known in the family—he was my great-great-grandfather—reputedly caused the 1906 earthquake in a contest of power with another medicine man. Like other medicine men and women from central California and beyond, Grandpa Tom, a Coast Miwok, used charmstones—oblong objects carved from quartz or various other hard rocks—when doctoring the sick, for luck in fishing and hunting, and for who knows what else—perhaps even causing an earthquake.

Mabel McKay witnessed a Lake County Indian doctor pulling a tiny rabbit from a sick woman's chest using a thumb-sized quartz charmstone; Mabel herself gave a troubled young man a charmstone to keep an evil spirit at bay. Maria Copa, a Coast Miwok born at Nicasio who sang for Tom Smith, told ethnographer Isabel Kelly that a charmstone had once followed a woman home and that the woman had to "hit it three times" with a stick to kill it. When American rancher William Bihler dynamited the southern end of Tolay Lake in the early 1870s, draining the rather large but shallow lake of water, what the muddy bottom revealed was thousands upon thousands of charmstones—far more than found in any one locale in North America.

Roughly seven miles east of Petaluma, Tolay is the southernmost and largest in a chain of lakes tucked within the Sonoma Mountains range. You might imagine it the pendant at the end of the chain. Standing on the ridges above the lake, you can see the emerald expanse of San Pablo Bay spreading before you and, like a sculpture rising from the water, San Francisco's Financial District, and then four of the Bay Area's major mountains: Mount Saint Helena, Mount Tamalpais, Mount Diablo, and Mount Burdell. All of the lakes in the chain were shallow, even more shallow than Tolay, hardly twenty feet in its deepest spot, but, like Tolay, all of the lakes contained water year-round, until after European contact, when the water table in the region dropped twenty to thirty feet in a relatively short period of time.

My ancestors occupied the region. Today we are known as the Federated Indians of Graton Rancheria, descendants of Natives identified by early ethnographers as Southern Pomo and Coast Miwok. These are names based on language families: Southern Pomo is a member of the Hokan family, and Coast Miwok belongs to the Penutian family. Southern Pomo, with its own various dialects, was spoken from the Santa Rosa plain north, and Coast Miwok was spoken southward to and including present-day Sausalito. But again, until recently, and for purposes of our relationship with the federal government, we never referred to ourselves as Pomo or Coast Miwok. We were over a dozen separate nation-states, each composed of between five hundred and two thousand individuals, and with one or more central villages and clearly defined national boundaries. Most people, regardless of their national affiliation, spoke several languages, some of them perhaps quite different from one another. Pomo is as different from Coast Miwok as English is from Urdu.

Tolay Lake is in the heartland of the Alaguali Nation, whose principal village, Cholequibit, sat southeast of the lake, bordering San Pablo Bay. The Alaguali knew their homeland intimately; typical of Coast Miwok and Southern Pomo nations, they practiced controlled burning, maintaining grasslands for elk and pronghorn, and they cleared waterways for fishing and hunting waterfowl, and cultivated sedge beds, growing long, straight roots for basket making. From the San Pablo marshes, they fished sturgeon and bat ray. Each nation, it seemed, had something unique that was needed by the others. A Southern Pomo nation near Santa Rosa mined obsidian prized for arrow-making. Southern Pomo and Coast Miwok along the Laguna de Santa Rosa grew the finest sedge, and the lagoon was full of perch and bass year-round. The Petaluma Nation's vast plains contained the largest herds of elk and deer. The Alaguali had the lake.

It wasn't only local indigenous nations who cherished the lake. Charmstones discovered in the lake bed came from a multitude of places throughout California, and from as far away as Mexico. Many are over four thousand years old. Certainly California Indians had extensive trade routes. More, the so-called discovery of these charmstones becomes evidence for the stories that continue to be passed down in our families. What we've always known is that Tolay Lake was a great place of healing and renewal, that Indian doctors came from near and far to confer with one another and to heal the sick. Members of a village at the southern end of the lake, not far from Cholequibit, hosted the visitors in several special houses made for fasting and ceremony.

Charmstones vary in length, but most are about two to three inches long, and most are oblong, although some are simply rounded. The specific shapes of others might suggest a phallic design, prompting some ethnographers and casual observers to think these charmstones were used in fertility rites. Sinkholes bored through some stones suggest they might've been used for fishing, specifically for anchoring nets. Whatever else charmstones may have been used for, they were used by medicine people to extract illness. The charmstone, in a sense, inherited the sickness, after which it had to be destroyed. Drowning was the usual method, whether in Tolay Lake or another body of water. Maria Copa's story reminds us that charmstones were considered living beings—they possessed living spirits like all elements of the material world. A person could also use a charmstone—and the sickness it took from an ill person—to harm another person.

Some of what we know about the Alaguali Nation and area comes from historical records, including those of the churches in the region. These records tell us that Father Abella, a Franciscan from Mission Dolores, baptized two elders from the village of Cholequibit in 1811, and Randall T. Milliken's meticulous study of mission records indicates that between 1811 and 1818, 151 Alagualic people were baptized—91 at Mission Dolores and 37 at Mission San José. Father José Altimira, traveling in 1823 from the Presidio in San Francisco to establish Mission San Francisco Solano in present-day Sonoma, stopped near the lake and noted in his journal that the surrounding hills would provide plenty of grass for cattle grazing and that the lake was named after "the chief of the Indians," called Tola.

The landscape, already altered, continued to change, in many places beyond the recognition of a person from just the generation before. The great herds of elk and pronghorn continued to disappear. Flocks of waterfowl, once rising from the waterways so thick as to block the sun, thinned. Native bunchgrasses, like purple needlegrass, were overrun by European oatgrass, spread from seeds in the dung of Spanish and Mexican livestock. After the missions were secularized in 1834, the Natives worked for General Vallejo on his Rancho Petaluma (which included Tolay Lake), mostly in some form of indentured servitude, tending his cattle and planting his crops.

It was no coincidence, although it was sadly ironic, that General Vallejo, defeated by Americans in the Bear Flag Revolt, helped California lawmakers draft, during their first legislative session in 1850, the Act for the Government and Protection of Indians, which legalized Indian slavery—a law that was not repealed in its entirety until 1937. Indians were separated from their families, but their aboriginal villages persevered, even as our population numbers dropped precipitously. We continued to eat many of our native foods, most notably acorn mush, and continued older religious practices. We made herculean efforts to maintain family connections, even as the aforementioned 1850 act provided loopholes for Americans to steal our children. J. B. Lewis, an American rancher who in the 1850s owned land north of Tolay Lake, noticed that Indians—he thought from a local tribe—"stayed a day or two [at the lake] and had some kind of powwow." It was only after William Bihler dynamited the southern end of the lake twenty years later that there were no reports of Indians returning.

At the time of European contact, the combined population of the Southern Pomo and Coast Miwok nations was about twenty thousand, although some estimates go much higher.

Central California, and the Bay Area in particular, was home to the densest population of indigenous peoples in North America outside of Mexico City, site of the ancient Aztec capital Tenochtitlan. Ethnographers have often wondered how so many people living so close together and speaking so many different languages got along with virtually little physical warfare for ten thousand years—yes, we've been here that long—but if you understand the cultures of those people, it's not so mysterious. From atop the ridges surrounding Tolay Lake, generation after generation of our people have watched the bay grow as it filled with water from the melting glacial ice caps. Believing that everything in nature is alive—and has power—you have to be careful not to mistreat or insult even the smallest pebble on your path. Likewise, people have power, often secret power. Secret songs, spirit guides, and objects such as charmstones protect a person and can be used against one's enemies. If you have to physically assault another person, you reveal that you have no secret power. Physical warfare thus is seen as the lowest form of war, since it suggests that you possess no spiritual power and can therefore be attacked without worry of retribution.

Ethnographers saw the culture as predicated on black magic and fear. Rather, the culture was predicated on profound respect: you had to be mindful of all life, reminded always that you were not the center of the universe but just a part of it. Sickness, whether caused by another human being or from a bird or a simple rock, dislocated one from the world, resulting in, if not continuing, imbalance. Medicine men and women drowned the charmstones to put away the sicknesses that were taken from their patients. The sickness was put away and the patient—and the natural world of which the patient was a part—was renewed. When the lake was drained of water and the old charmstones were exposed, did the Indians fear the return of all that sickness?

For the past several years, the Federated Indians of Graton Rancheria has held its summer picnic at Tolay Lake. We gather to enjoy food and reconnect with family. Booths offer information on language and basketry classes. At one booth, we can trace our ancestry to one or more of fourteen survivors from whom we all descend. Children can visit goats and chickens inside the restored barns. Hayrides take us across the dry lake bed and up onto the mountain ridges. Yet even as I give my welcoming speech as tribal chairman, extolling the virtue of our gathering again in a sacred place, I've often wondered if it is such a good idea for us to be here. Members of the Cardoza family, who once owned the ranch, gathered charmstones as they planted pumpkins, leaving the lake bed bare—and for a long time they displayed the stones in buckets during the Fall Festival. Even if the charmstones no longer hold disease and sickness, might not those things remain in the soil, or in the humid air that rises from the restored lake?

On hayrides, I watch as relatives and friends point from the ridgetops and name ancient villages. "There," a young woman says, looking south below the lake. "Cholequibit. The priest baptized a man and his wife there and named them Isidro and Isidra. They are my ancestors." Another young woman looks west and points. "Olumpali. My ancestors are from there. The priest baptized them Otilio and Otilia." So many of our people have been lost as a consequence of an ugly history. Too many have lived—often difficult lives—and died with little sense of the homeland, much less of the sacred lake. Seeing these young women and others, some of whom are taking in the views for the first time, I understand something about renewal—about what must have occurred as Indian doctors and their patients left the lake. Didn't the ridgetop views confirm that healing had occurred, that one was located in place again? Even if Grandpa Smith didn't return to the lake after it was drained, might not he have climbed a ridge to remember Petaluma, the birthplace of his mother?

During a lull in this past winter's endless rain, I went to Tolay. The lake collects water during the winter months, and with the abundant rain, I thought I might see the lake as it once was—or maybe close to what it once was. Archaeologists have noted that the lake's southern membrane was thin, suggesting that people of Alaguali maintained a dam, no doubt regulating waterflow from the lake. I found the water was high, extending from just below the farms' barns to the opposite end of the valley below the hills. A lone osprey flew overhead. Mud hens and mallards bobbed on the muddy water. Under a cloudy sky, I stood and tossed a small piece of angelica root into the water to appease the spirits. I figured if the lake's ridges helped locate my people, then the story of the lake and its charmstones can remind us again of the power within all life. Yes, I thought, imbue reverence.

Then, as I was walking back to my car parked behind the gate above the lake, I began to wonder about my people who might not believe the story. And what of non-Indians who haven't yet heard it? Might not fooling around at the lake be dangerous? Thinking has its clever way of taking me out of the moment, and here I was thinking again, lost. Until I reached my car. It was then that the sky opened and silvery sunlight covered the land around me. The four mountains in the distance remained in shadow and seemed to grow out of the land like huge fingers. The lake was below me, flat and broad. All at once I understood something else, or rather I felt it. In that brief moment before the clouds shielded the sun again, I felt what it was like to be held. I was standing in the earth's enormous hand.

OSPREY TALKS TO ME ONE DAY

Remember a place along the river. Recall the season, the time of day, how the sun shone on the water, the trees' shadows. Wohler Bridge. 1972. Midsummer. Midday. On a sandy beach where the river bends just before meeting the bridge. I am twenty years old, alone. Clear water ripples like beveled glass; small fish, no doubt carp, tease and dart at the shore. But what's caught my attention is a single silver osprey, a bird I've noticed coursing the river countless times before, hovering now midair above me.

On weekends sunbathers, mostly young, carve out spots, a patch of sand, maybe under a shady willow, to drink beer and smoke weed. And, yes, to swim naked. They park in an empty lot below the bridge and hike north. But I knew of this place long before, when, as an even younger man, I accompanied Pomo basket maker and medicine woman Mabel McKay to pick herbs and cut willow branches for basket making. I remember paper bags filled with mountain balm—for asthma, Mabel said—and I can still see the armfuls of straight willow branches tied with strips of colored cloth that we hauled back to her car, parked under a redwood near the bridge.

Mabel was a Lake County Pomo. It was her good friend Essie Parrish, a medicine woman like Mabel, who first told her of this place. Essie Parrish, like others of her generation from Southern Pomo tribes, knew the Russian River well, its nooks and crannies, where to fish, where to gather herbs. "Medicine growing," Mabel called the place, perhaps using Essie's name for it.

The indigenous people did not think of the river as a 110-mile body of water, as a geographer might. They didn't conceive of it as a single unit or phenomenon but rather as a continuum of interconnected places, no different from the way they understand all features of the wider landscape, each with its own character and story. The storied landscape thus is a sacred text, an outcropping of rocks, a mountain peak, the river mouth, all mnemonic pegs reminding us not only of the world we find ourselves in but of how to live harmoniously with it.

Except for the Coast Miwok, located south of the river, the indigenous nations of this area are Pomo. Both terms—

Coast Miwok and Pomo—are linguistic classifications, but we belonged to at least a dozen distinct nations with distinct territories. Sometimes a nation's people were identified by the name of the central village, as with the *Peta · luma*, which translates to sloping ridge, after a prominent feature of the landscape. The Kashaya Pomo called the part of the river near present-day Jenner *Shabaiki*, or south water place, and one Southern Pomo nation referred to a place near present-day Healdsburg as *Ashokawa*, east water place. Other locales were associated with fish and animals. Coho Salmon House. Grizzly Bear Path. Rattlesnake Coming Out.

Villages, indeed entire nations, were organized and located around bodies of water. Creeks. Lakes. The Santa Rosa lagoon. The Russian River. Each nation was responsible for the health of its water. Willows had to be cut back, lest falling branches clog the water, impede its flow. Sedge was maintained for the same reason. Since all bodies of water connect to one another throughout the territory of at least twelve distinct independent nations, each with between five hundred and two thousand individuals, the health of the water was also indicative of the well-being between nations. If nations in the foothills did not take care of their creeks, ensuring clean, free-flowing water for migrating fish to spawn, the nations located near river marshes forbade them to dig for the water potatoes that grew in the marshes. Likewise, if the marsh reeds and river trails were neglected, the hill nations wouldn't trade for the herbs and flint for arrow-making that can be found only in the hills. Dozens of large creeks join the river, including the Maacama Creek east of Healdsburg, along which numerous indigenous villages were located. A healthy river meant peace.

In a clean river, fish were abundant. Steelhead. White Sturgeon the size of small whales. Spawning salmon so thick at the mouth of the river that a person could cross to the other side on their shiny black backs. Mostly people fished with nets. "Get your nets ready," tribal leaders would call as the fish began to migrate upstream. There were abundant animals too, including beavers and sea otters not seen today or only rarely. Porpoises frolicked upriver as far inland as Guerneville. Seals always camped on the river shore near the ocean, competing with people and grizzly bears for fish, especially salmon.

Oh, and there are so many stories . . . Near Jenner a young Pomo was leeching acorns in the sand. Busy talking to another woman also leeching acorns, she lost track of her young son, who'd found his way upriver, not too far from his mother but out of her sight. This was on the north side of the river, where today cattle graze on green grass that meets the water.

When she found the boy near the river, she was startled to see a huge white sturgeon head sticking up out of the water, appearing ready to swallow the boy on the shore. Luckily, she reached him in time. But then, not long after she got home (she left her acorn meal in the sand), her son fell into a coma. When the medicine man came in from work (the villagers were living on a ranch, tending sheep and cattle for a white man), he prayed over the boy.

"What did you see?" the medicine man asked the boy when he woke.

"An old man in the river," the boy answered. "He told me he was lonely for his people. There weren't many left."

"Yes," the medicine man said. He turned to the boy's mother. "He didn't want to eat your son. He was telling him that he can't forget his people. What happened to the fish can happen to us, too."

My family traces its history to the river. As indigenous people in Sonoma and Mendocino Counties, we all do. My great-great-great-grandmother, Tsupu (baptized Maria Checca), was born near *Peta · luma*, sloping ridge. Her father was born in a village on Mark West Creek, which joins the Russian River north of Forestville. Her son, who was Tom Smith, would later build his ceremonial Roundhouse on the Jenner Head. There he preached about the importance of remembering our traditions, the rules of living with the land. Pointing to the river, he said, "Like that water, we are connected to everything. It's memory." His granddaughter, my grandmother, sat below the redwoods at Wohler Bridge watching cockfights with her friends and relatives.

Filipino farmworkers, the *manongs*, hosted the fights. A large bonfire was built. They wore their best clothes—pinstriped suits, gold chains, Panama hats—never mind the spurting blood, mostly to impress the single Indian girls gathered for the fight. My grandmother said the bonfires were so big you could see the illuminated tops of the tall trees from across the river. An anti-miscegenation law forbade Filipino men marriage licenses in California at the time, and American Indians were some of the only women available to these young bachelors brought from the Philippines to work on farms and in kitchens. Today, there is a significant amount of Filipino ancestry in the tribes. My grandmother, for instance, married my Filipino grandfather in 1929 (in Tijuana, so she could have a marriage license), and although they lived in Los Angeles, she returned with him to the Russian River area to visit family and friends, and one of the best places to find them was at the Wohler Bridge cockfights, located, coincidentally, where

I parked my car before heading up the river to swim. In 1972, I didn't know about the cockfights. I would learn about them from my grandfather and other *manongs*.

My grandmother, who I didn't know, comes alive in a story. I see her by the bonfire, roosters at each other midair, just as I see, from another story, a small Indian boy and, hardly a foot away, the face of a fish large as a whale. I see salmon plentiful enough that I can walk across them like a bridge. I see sea otters wrestling on a muddy shore, and beaver dams the size of houses atop the water. I see clean water . . . And me now. 1972. Wohler Bridge. A warm summer day. I start to peel off my clothes to swim. But then I stop, looking back up at the magnificent silver bird still hovering above me. "I know the river," the bird says. "Follow me," and already I'm in the sky able to see below me the length of the river and a hundred places I can land.

AFTER THE FALL

On December 19, 1913, the Hetch Hetchy Valley disappeared. With the stroke of a pen, President Woodrow Wilson signed the congressional bill that authorized the construction of the O'Shaughnessy Dam. Ten years later, the Hetch Hetchy—seven miles long and up to one mile wide, Yosemite's northern twin—started to flood.

More than one hundred years later, the decision still haunts. In 1987, Secretary of the Interior Donald Hodel proposed tearing the dam down, but nothing came of it. The State of California has studied the costs and benefits of restoring the valley, and even if the studies prove correct that removing the dam may not be complicated, it's much harder to believe it will actually happen. I have studied the environmental reports and historical documents, looked at the computer-generated designs, and read the journals of one of the valley's earliest chroniclers, John Muir, and then begun to imagine.

August 2033
SPIRITS

The massive lake shrinks; 360,000 acre-feet of impounded water begins to disappear. Stumps from giant oaks felled nearly a hundred years ago appear beneath the surface like shadows. What spirits rise?

Big news: After years of maneuvering, Congress authorizes the restoration of the Hetch Hetchy Valley. With pomp and circumstance, a formal ceremony will take place in four months, on December 19, the one hundredth anniversary of the Raker Act, which allowed San Francisco to build the O'Shaughnessy Dam and flood the valley. But already restoration has begun; the water is receding. The granite cliffs grow taller.

Noontime. I am perched on a large boulder below Wapama Falls—a mere mossy dribble on this August day. In the shade of a madrone, my company: a scraggly pine on the cliff above, a stoic observer; and, flitting branch to branch in a nearby oak, a blue-tailed scrub jay breaking the warm stillness with a periodic squawk.

Little in the landscape indicates change thus far; nothing portends the future. The water level has dropped ten feet, only slightly widening the watermark—that swath of bleached granite—surrounding the lake. Still, birds sing, trees and rocks absorb the sun. Across the lake's glass, a motionless surface, the immense rock Kolana, two thousand feet higher than the valley's floor, stands like a sentinel clocking summer's slow progress to autumn.

And the place—the granite walls, the flooded valley— begins to speak with a multitude of voices, a complex history— peoples, plants, animals, even water—rising, and the past is all I have. My Miwok ancestors said not to mention the dead. If spirits attempt to speak, they said, run. But the world is upside down. Spirits in this emptying place are all I have. What else can I do but consider them?

John Muir speaks to me. He saw what no one living has seen—the valley before it was drowned: "The pines sway dreamily, and you are shoulder-deep in grass and flowers. . . . The sublime rocks of its walls seem to glow with life . . . while birds, bees, and butterflies help the river and waterfalls to stir all the air into music." He called it "a grand landscape garden."

He first visited Hetch Hetchy in 1871. But he wasn't the first non-Native visitor; nor was the garden exactly as the Natives had known it. For at least twenty years cattle and horses from the westerly foothills had roamed into the valley, grazing and dropping dung loaded with non-native seed stock. The shoulder-deep grass Muir speaks of was no doubt wild oat, a species that supplanted native grasses everywhere in California. Birds likewise aided the spread of foreign grass and plant species.

Before Muir: Joseph Screech, the first European known to have seen the valley, was a mere passing hunter in 1850. "Mere," I say, for Hetch Hetchy, like its southern twin, Yosemite, was "discovered" in 1851 by James Savage, who led the Mariposa Battalion on a mission to capture the Ahwahneechee, a tribe of resistant Sierra Miwok who had raided his trading post on the Fresno River before fleeing into the hills.

The discovery, thus, was an accident of war, as it was nearly fifty years earlier when an expedition of Spanish soldiers, sent from Mission San Juan Bautista to explore the territory as a possible locale for a new mission, was overwhelmed near this spot by a siege of monarch butterflies—*mariposas* in Spanish. Father Pedro Muñoz, who accompanied the soldiers and kept a journal, wrote that the creatures became "extremely trouble-some," aggressive, so thick in numbers that "they obscure[d] the light of the sun." Today the county is named Mariposa.

Later, the Spaniards came upon several abandoned villages along the Merced River. The Native inhabitants, except for an old woman left behind, had fled into the hills, well ahead of the soldiers. When the soldiers approached, the old woman jumped into the rushing water and fought efforts to rescue her.

The Sierra Club's dream is to return Hetch Hetchy to its native splendor. It will take between 80 and 120 years, they say, to see their vision come to fruition—the reservoir emptied; O'Shaughnessy Dam completely removed; the Tuolumne River again free; the valley floor open, seven miles long, from one-fourth to half a mile wide.

The plan, outlined in a National Park Service report in 1988, calls for a phased drawdown of the reservoir to manage the revegetation and reintroduction of animals. Each year, countless native trees and shrubs will be planted and fenced—at least five hundred black oaks and a combined subtotal of four hundred white alder, black cottonwood, Douglas fir, dogwood, willows, azaleas, manzanitas, and ceanothus. Likewise with the addition of animals—foxes, bighorn sheep, bobcats, and a wide variety of bird species (although no wolves or grizzly bears, since the latter is extinct and no one knows whether or not the wolf was ever an inhabitant of the area).

The Park Service's plan was drawn largely from Muir's observations, as well as some later photographs and paintings by others. Digital recreations show Muir's majestic vistas: "the oaks assembled in magnificent groves with massive rugged trunks four to six feet in diameter, and broad, shady, wide-spreading heads. The shrubs forming conspicuous flowering clumps and tangles are manzanita, azalea, spiraea, brier-rose, several species of ceanothus, calycanthus, philadelphus, wild cherry, etc.; with abundance of showy and fragrant herbaceous plants growing about them or out in the open beds by themselves—lilies, Mariposa tulips, brodiaeas, orchids, iris, . . .larkspur, columbine, goldenrods, sunflowers, mints of many species. . ."

I have to shut my eyes to see it. Today the hills are dry, a uniform straw color interrupted only by the green of occasional oaks and pines and, farther below, the ashen gray of granite.

Then the flat sea of water.

Shortly after I arrived this morning, I spotted a lone peregrine falcon circling over the lake. I was excited, thinking somehow the bird was an omen of great things, of stupendous finds, insight even. My plan was to traverse the circumference of the reservoir, stepping off the dam and starting along the eastern walls past Kolana, and then coming back west. Counterclockwise, the holy direction for the Sierra Miwok. But trails ended short, and steep cliffs made further travel impossible. Maybe the park ranger at the gate was right: "Not much to see at this point."

But spirits.

Totoya, she's another. Odd that she is the last I hear, but no wonder: she is the last Miwok to have memory of Yosemite—and presumably Hetch Hetchy—before European contact. She was the granddaughter of Tenaya, the Ahwahneechee chief who surrendered to Savage. One of her granddaughters had a son under a tree by a stream in the still-open valley, then later abandoned the child to relatives before marrying a dam builder.

Caretakers and destroyers married. And on April 20, 1931, Totoya—later called Maria Lebrado—died, not long after Hetch Hetchy was flooded.

As for the future: agents, all of us, to undo and restore, undrown and retrieve. What picture then? What story?

Might my companions—the stoic pine, the noisy jay—know something more than us, as if Hetch Hetchy were itself a single grand oak cracked apart, and this ring of bleached granite along its walls a chronicle of the one-hundred-year flood? And the lone peregrine falcon this morning, was it seeing rabbits and squirrels beneath the lake's glossy surface?

June 2053
MUSINGS

Tourists gather at the Visitor Center, which is modeled after an Indian Roundhouse. Much larger in scale—four hundred feet in diameter, three stories high—its granite-gray walls look impenetrable. But inside, light pours from floor-to-ceiling transparent panes, lending the place an open, cathedral-like feel.

You don't have to think here. Dozens of TV monitors tell you where you have been—the parking lot—and where you are going—the course of the park tour. You can know everything, including, for example, why you and your vehicle were so carefully scrutinized with X-ray cameras upon entry. (The park is hypervigilant for environmental contaminants—oil on tires or the soles of your shoes—and invasive species—seeds in uncooked trail mix, a single spore attached to a pant leg.)

On one screen there is a digitized history of Hetch Hetchy. I maneuver the film quickly forward, past the dismantling of O'Shaughnessy Dam and the present, to what I'll never see: Muir's Eden, sixty years yet to come.

Outside, the mid-morning light is bright. Park guides lead tours through the valley. Park gardeners work in its groves and flower beds. Ten of us collect on a wide platform that overlooks the valley. Our guide provides a brief overview of what we'll see, in case we hadn't gleaned as much from the monitors. He is twentysomething, enthusiastic. He explains the rules, too: essentially that we mustn't wander from the group or touch anything without first asking. His talk is peppered with environmental truisms and buzzwords. Survival of the wisest. Collectivize. Interrelate. Connect.

It's been thirty years since my first visit. My ancestral homeland today: undrowned.

The long view is magnificent. The falls against the valley's northern walls, Tueeulala and Wapama, are as Muir saw them: the former "waving like a downy scarf, silver bright, burning with white sun-fire in every fiber"; the latter, a short distance east, "thundering and beating in a shadowy gorge." The freed Tuolumne River winds along, a ribbon of light, its banks dotted with clumps of willow and cottonwood. Orchards of oaks cluster farther from the river; and, spreading from the trees in every direction, carpeting the valley floor, flowers: a patchwork of purples, pinks, and yellows. Lupines and Mariposa tulips, goldenrods and sunflowers.

Our first stop is the nursery. Plexiglas hothouses protect peat beds of countless seedlings to be transplanted—grasses, plants, trees. Chicken-coop-like barns shelter birds and animals, fledglings and the infirm. Our guide gloats over three California condor chicks huddled under a heat lamp. We learn the condor was the last native bird to be introduced. The helpless chicks look like skinned rodents rolled in dandelion down.

The nursery was well-camouflaged behind a wall of pines. We didn't see it from the platform that overlooks the valley. Likewise, as we round a prominent granite cliff, traveling below the northern walls, the nursery disappears. Yet lower in the valley, closer to the river, signs of human intervention appear again: leaf-green nets draped over trees and across flower beds; mesh fences that enclose marshes. The park's "intensive management program" at work.

On the trail, we pass gardeners pushing wooden carts carrying young plants and tools, shovels and such. They wear earth-toned uniforms and pay little attention to us, even when we stand sometimes only ten feet away as our guide explains what they're doing: planting brodiaea bulbs, trimming deadwood from a copse of Douglas fir, mapping with white flags a stretch of grass and unwanted fir and cedar saplings for the next prescribed burn.

We hike back out of the valley, then rest below Wapama Falls. It's a remarkable view south across the river and flat meadows to mighty Kolana, something I couldn't have imagined thirty years ago. The open landscape, a young—not yet bald—bald eagle soaring overhead, two fat pronghorn feeding on manzanita bark just below us.

Our guide notes that restoration is on schedule. Boundaries for most aboriginal plant communities have been established, some are stabilizing. Many of the trees have not reached their full height—the Douglas firs and incense cedars need another forty years—but everything is in place.

As proof, he takes a folded reprint of a painting from his shirt pocket and asks us—shouting over the booming falls—to pass it around. The artist was William Keith, who, on a trip with Muir in 1907, painted the view a year later. Indeed blotches of purple are in the same spot below Kolana: lupines. Yellow too, by a bend in the river: buttercups and sunflowers. Alders and cottonwoods and willows are where they should be; azaleas below the pines and dense ceanothus on the rocky rises.

Muir remained optimistic after Congress passed the Raker Act in 1913, proclaiming, "Fortunately, wrong cannot last; soon or late it must fall back home to Hades, while some compensating good must surely follow."

The battle for Hetch Hetchy was the first one Americans

took against growth and development. It galvanized the Sierra Club, transforming a hiking association into arguably the nation's most powerful conservation organization. The Sierra Club, one hundred years after the Raker Act, got back Hetch Hetchy—certainly a "compensating good."

But it is not easy or perfect. Nor has it ever been. Strife persists. Nature's strange dynamism is beyond our control. Two hundred years ago, wild oats overtook the native purple needlegrass and clover. Later, Savage's battalion colonized the Sierra Miwok. Today, blackbirds and starlings are sworn enemies. Deer and bighorn sheep wreak havoc on newly planted grass; raccoons retrieve reintroduced fish from the marshes.

Is there ever an end to nets and fences?

From here, above the valley floor, you can't see these barricades. It's a view, like Muir's and Keith's, that presumes an absence of human intervention, of history. The landscape seems virgin. The viewer can even forget—or certainly not be reminded of—his presence and effect on the land. Even Lafayette Bunnell, a member of the Mariposa Battalion who kept a memoir in which he described the bloody battles, also remarked on the landscape's majestic beauty. We marvel at all we see.

Of course we now know the limits of the dream to restore Hetch Hetchy. There's no shoulder-deep grass here, and there never will be. We compromise and mutter: easier to break something than to fix it.

My Miwok ancestors cultivated the oak groves. They gathered acorns, yes, but each fall they also raked away old leaves and nuts to prevent moth larvae from destroying the trees. They planted bulbs and thinned sedge along the marshes for better harvests. Seems a relative harmony.

But they had to learn. Archaeological records indicate instances of environmental plunder, which included the destruction of entire herds of buffalo over cliffs in Montana, and overfishing—to the point of extinction—varieties of clams and mussels on the Pacific Coast. And they did not just learn but developed stories that shaped for them—always reminding them of—the necessity for a shared existence with the natural world. But those Indians had millenniums to learn; we don't. The oceans rise. Glaciers that lined the spine of South America are completely gone. Deserts grow. Forests shrink. Invading species, new diseases. In the last century, war forced the migration of untold millions. This century the culprit is environmental neglect.

No one here naively enjoys the view. No one came here for that. None of us is different. We've learned to hope. It's an informed and urgent hope. We know all the words for nets and fences and know that if a better story isn't made here, it won't be made anywhere.

June 2123
THE GARDEN

Grandfather

I sit below Wapama Falls; perhaps I'm on the same boulder where you sat when you first visited. Same company, too: a squawking jay; a scraggly pine, stoic observer on the cliff above. But what I see you only imagined.

Here they are again, the oaks with "massive rugged trunks four to six feet in diameter" in full splendor, magnificent, each grove an immense edifice, a palace on the valley floor. Dwellings of willow and cottonwood and alder overlook the gold-lit Tuolumne and its bogs and marshes. Purples and yellows glow so intense in this light you'd think the flowers—irises, lupines, goldenrods, and sunflowers—had swallowed a share of the sun.

Bighorn sheep travel east below Kolana, blending with the landscape but for their white rears. Below me, a deer exits her cover of manzanita; two fawns with faded white spots follow. What's in the low brush I can't tell—a coyote waking for its nighttime prowl, chipmunks, lizards?

Oh, and the birds. Close to me, in addition to the jay, are a pileated woodpecker mounting the trunk of a sugar pine, and smaller birds darting about the brush: finches, sparrows and wrens. Doves flap overhead, going north to roosts higher in the hills. A pair of peregrine falcons twirl and dive in the distance, not hunting but joyously playing, if not merely boasting their skill in the air. A condor glides in this direction from Kolana. Its shadow across the valley floor is the size of a small airplane.

Five feet away is a bear trail. It leads east past the falls, then north over the cliffs and out of the valley. Black bears have been back in Hetch Hetchy for years. They feed on the lush berry gardens and eat pine nuts and acorns. They are timid generally and hide, though sometimes in the evening you can find them on their way into the valley to feed.

The world reveres this place. It's a university with keys— stories, Grandfather—to our continued survival on the planet. Its natural libraries are the richest. Scholars worldwide come here looking for clues to replicate its beauty and harmony.

We know some important answers. There isn't—and never will be—a virgin garden. Lest this work, this living museum, be diminished, human intervention is necessary, as you suspected, Grandfather. We are a part, not apart, and we play a role. Plant and animal communities have stabilized—yes, ponderosa pines and incense cedars are 125 to 150 feet high—but require constant attention.

Cameras the size of eraser heads strategically located in trees and cliffs monitor every creature, each blossom and blade of grass, all of which are accounted for in a master computer that helps determine any tension among species, overcrowding as well as undercrowding.

Removal of an extra raccoon or blue fox is simple and relatively painless. Inside each camera is a pin-sized stun gun that emits electronic rays to temporarily sedate the animal until park gardeners can retrieve and relocate it.

Paths lead everywhere. Off the main trail that circles the valley you can explore shady canyons, see ferns six feet high, walk through bright meadows to the river, watch minnows bustle under the reeds.

I arrived early this morning, wanting a full day here. I walked, yes counterclockwise, starting below Kolana and completing a journey, Grandfather, you never could. On your last trip here tours traversed only the northern side of the valley. And today no guides are necessary. A chip placed in your cellphone provides a detailed map. A flashing green light indicates your precise location with respect to the Visitor

Center—and allows it in turn to know your whereabouts—and a voice can guide you back or farther on according to your wishes. You can't follow the "bathtub ring" any longer: it is all but gone, visible only in occasional spots, highlighted by the almost unnatural mauves and chartreuses of the younger lichen.

It's a joy to travel alone, stopping and pondering the landscape as I wished: a bed of pink orchids below the ferns, Mariposa tulips completely circling a marsh. I followed an eagle's path, my head tilted back, until I was dizzy.

Of particular interest to me are the edible plants. Cities grow them in parks. Families plant backyards and front yards with them. There are many varieties of oak here, in addition to the grand black oaks, for acorns—a food many in California and elsewhere eat regularly. There are also bulbs, such as brodiaeas and tule potatoes, healthful carbohydrate sources, and rosehips for vitamin C. Soaproot is not just for shampooing hair but for fishing—using the mashed bulb to intoxicate fish.

Alongside a vast pond at the far end of the valley, sometime past noon, before I headed back in this direction, I watched park gardeners waist-deep in the water pulling up "Indian potatoes" from below the tules with their bare feet. Though they wore wetsuits—and had modern-cut hair, various colors—I thought of our Miwok ancestors who had harvested the tubers the same way for ten thousand years.

In 1854, a Belgian miner named Perlot helped the defeated Ahwahneechee by arranging a treaty with the local white settlers. Later, he wrote: "But who can tell us that the progress of civilization will not bring us to the point where the Indian is."

Such ruefulness will never be escaped.

Only today, the big news here is the sighting of a grizzly bear, the park's only unwanted aboriginal inhabitant. It's come out of nowhere—a thousand miles away, from the southern reaches of Montana?—as if the restored valley, missing the creature, called it home.

Once they were as numerous here as people. Muir suggested that there was a kind of agreement between them and the Natives when Hetch Hetchy was, in Muir's words, a home and stronghold of the Tuolumne Indians, as Ahwahne was of the grizzlies. Indeed, throughout Native California the grizzly was respected as the most powerful character of the landscape, both symbol and embodiment of nature's capacity—stronger than any human capacity—for both evil and good.

Of course park officials' first concern is safety. Uncertainty exists as to whether or not the electronic guns are powerful enough to stun the animal should a gardener or tourist be in danger, never mind how the species might affect the valley's restored ecology.

I stopped here because of that bear. This the place you viewed the valley from, and I've been here a number of times. No, I'm not tempting fate. In a moment I'll leave safely. But sitting on this rock, amid the deafening falls and in the lengthening shadows, I gaze up the bear trail, beyond walls of laurel and into the darkness, thinking: This is how the first story started and maybe the last.

TREES

THE ANCIENT ONES

There was a woman who wanted to teach me love medicine. Well, there was a man before her, but she was the first to give me a song and ingredients, the most potent of which, in addition to quail droppings, was the golden red pitch from a redwood tree. The older the tree, the better; the pitch from an old tree is richer, more powerful, principally because, as this woman had told me, it contains a longer memory of the forest.

Descriptions of indigenous peoples' use of the redwood tree abound. Coastal redwoods, the tallest and among the oldest trees on earth, are unique to a relatively narrow stretch of land bordering the coast from what we call today southern Oregon down to the Monterey Peninsula. Dozens of indigenous nations inhabited—and still inhabit—the region. Surely these people and their distinct cultures coevolved with the magnificent trees. The Yurok and Wiyot of northwestern California split square planks from the trees' durable wood for their houses, and from the same hard wood they crafted seafaring canoes. The deep, swift-moving Klamath River was an important travel route for many of the northwestern California Indian nations, and only canoes dug out from the trunks of heavy redwood ensured safety crossing the river and traveling its great length. My people, the Southern Pomo and Coast Miwok of Sonoma and Marin Counties, removed slabs of bark from the trees and leaned the slabs against a center pole to build conical houses, called *kotchas* by the Coast Miwok. Southern Pomo called the slabs of bark *cashi-da*, house skin. Smaller slabs were used to construct acorn granaries, the hard, impenetrable redwood protecting the acorns from pests and rodents and keeping them free from mildew. The hollow of a redwood trunk could also be used to store acorns, as long as the damp ground was covered by rocks and a layer of bay laurel leaves. Young children made dolls from the hairy bark. In his *Ethnographic Notes on the Southwestern Pomo* (1967), ethnographer James Gifford noted even more uses: "The new foliage, warmed in the fire, was applied as a poultice for earache. The gummy sap which accumulated at the bottom of a hollow redwood was also taken as medicine for a run-down condition. It was soaked in water and the liquid was drunk as a tonic."

Nowhere in any of the literature I've read, however, is there mention of the sap used for love medicine. "You mustn't tell anyone we are talking about this," the woman said to me, I felt as much to warn me as to see if I could be trusted.

I was an adult, in my forties, and I knew better. I shouldn't have let myself get into this position with her in the first place. Worse, when she had broached the subject, I'd encouraged her: I listened.

"Listen," she began. "When I was a young woman, my husband left me for another woman—a girl up north who was much prettier than me. And he was unkind about it. He told me, 'You, girl, aren't pretty. I will get tired of you. Her, I'll never be able to get enough of.' Shortly thereafter, my old aunt, who knew what happened, approached me. 'You want him back?' she asked. She already knew my answer—and I already knew what she could teach me. It was raining hard, I remember. She looked out the window at the rain—we were living on the old reservation—and she said, 'In four days there will be sun. Then we will go to the redwoods. We will go to the redwoods first where it is dark at noon.'"

I got caught by her story. I'd heard rumors about this woman, about the dangerous powers she possessed. "Don't take anything to eat or drink from her," a relative warned. "Don't let her get a strand of your hair." The old-timers—

and still a few Indians today—use the term *poison* for medicine that can cause ill effects in another, whether that means making one act against one's will or causing sickness or even death. Sometimes a person like that would use charmstones. To cast a spell, a poisoner might touch you with the charmstone or simply point it in your direction. A poisoner might also have a song, or a series of songs referred to as "mates." Often, casting a spell required a combination of things: powerful objects, songs, and herbs and other substances taken from the plant world. The first person who offered to teach me love medicine was an old man who lived in town, around the corner from Indian friends I'd been visiting. He'd extended his hand to me, and resting on his open palm was a beautifully polished green oblong stone.

Ethnographers, archaeologists, and the like have their theories of how our people came to this continent. One popular story is that we migrated over the Bering Strait ten thousand years ago, during the last ice age. Theories also get revised. Skeletal remains found in Central America suggest we were here twenty thousand years before the Bering Strait was crossable, and recent discoveries of crudely manufactured tools in Florida and San Diego suggest our ancestors lived here in small tribes at the same time the Neanderthal inhabited caves in southern France. But who's counting?

While studying the language of the Kashaya Pomo in the late 1950s, UC Berkeley linguist Robert Oswalt collected a story from a tribal elder telling of a time when the ocean rose and a whale lived at the mouth of the Gualala River. The coastal people retreated from the rising water and, traveling inland to high mountains, settled in caves until the water receded. Oswalt translated the story into English and classified it in his study, *Kashaya Texts* (1964), as a myth. A few years later, geologists studying the river basin discovered the fossil remains of a whale that dated back ten thousand years, to when the same river basin was an inland ocean bay. Carbon-dated materials, such as charcoal found in the caves of Northern California's Mount Saint Helena, indicate people lived in the caves at or near the same time. Did we once look west from the mountaintop and watch the redwoods return above the water?

But of course the redwoods were here long before we were. Fossil records indicate that relatives of today's redwoods existed 160 million years ago, during the Jurassic era; some scientists interpret the data differently and suggest the trees' ancestors were here 240 million years ago. Most agree that redwoods have been in their present range, from southern Oregon to the Monterey Peninsula, for at least 20 million years. And this is the only place on earth the redwood trees are found—trees that can live for two thousand years and reach heights of over three hundred feet. They no doubt loomed large in the ancient cultures of aboriginal Californians.

In the northwestern and central regions of the state, we belonged to small nations of between one thousand and five thousand individuals, each nation often comprised of subgroups of related families. At the time of European contact, in the mid 1700s, there were more people in central California than anywhere else in the New World outside of the Aztec capital, Tenochtitlan, the site of present-day Mexico City, and numerous languages were spoken across the region. Most language families found in the New World as a whole were at some point found in California, and it wasn't unusual for a person to be conversant in several dialects, each one from a distinct language group. Coast Miwok is a member of the Penutian language family, for instance, whereas Pomo is a Hokan language, as dissimilar from Coast Miwok as English is from Urdu. Villagers across the creek might speak a completely different language from their nearest neighbors.

Because national territories were small—and boundaries strictly observed—tribes took great care not only of their relationships with other groups of people but also of their relationship with the land. No part of the landscape was unknown to aboriginal Californians, and they managed their resources carefully. We knew where quail nested, and we kept waterways clear of brush for ducks and geese, both to encourage the migratory waterfowl to nest and to make hunting them easier. Sedge roots were thinned and pruned to grow longer, stronger fibers for basket making, and the land was regularly burned for a variety of reasons related to the plants and animals we depended on for survival. One of the first laws the Spanish explorers and settlers imposed on us was against controlled burning, as they believed we were setting the land on fire to starve their livestock. In fact, we practiced controlled burning for a number of reasons, one of the most important being for the health of the oak trees, which gave us the acorn, our staple food. Fire destroyed larvae on the ground that would otherwise become moths that would infest the acorns and decimate the harvest. We also used controlled burning to enrich grasslands for herds of elk, pronghorn, and deer that thrived on open plains and hillsides, and we burned to control underbrush, not only so that grasslands and large trees might thrive but also to prevent wildfires we could not control.

And here I have to pause. Only two weeks before I began

writing this essay, I was evacuated from my home on Sonoma Mountain at the beginning of the historic North Bay firestorm that claimed more than 150,000 acres across Sonoma, Napa, and Solano Counties in October 2017. Over nine thousand structures were lost, including three thousand homes in Santa Rosa alone. Forty-four people died. The fire burned young redwood trees, but the region's ancient trees, located out of the fire's range, were unaffected. My father's cousin, a woman near ninety, offered, "Them trees won't go, don't worry. They ain't going anyplace. They been here long as us—and they'll be here long as us." Scars on old-growth trees and stumps show the trees have withstood fires before. The thick bark and hard, decay-resistant wood—one of the features that made the trees so attractive to early American loggers—protects them not only from fire and flood but also from disease. No known insect can destroy a redwood tree. Even when a tree is severely damaged, or even cut down, clones often sprout from the base, and the same tree is then able to live again and again.

The Natives in the coastal regions of central California—I'm thinking principally of my people, the Southern Pomo and Coast Miwok—seldom ventured far into the redwood forests. For a host of reasons, we regarded the tall trees with great respect, even fear. The forests were so dense, the trees so tall, that before long you could find yourself in total darkness. Amidst countless and similar-looking trunks, you might quickly become lost, unable to see a way out. The dark forests were home to grizzly bears, the most powerful creatures of the land and, at that time, more numerous than people. Other animals knew as much and stayed away. Settlers discovered that they could rush elk and pronghorn to the line of a redwood forest for easy slaughter because the animals would not go into the trees. The Southern Pomo word for a redwood tree is *qasil*. For the forest, often a simple noun is used: *du-weli*, meaning night.

The landscape was our sacred text, and we listened to what it told us. Everywhere you looked there were stories. An outcropping of rocks was what had become of a greedy man's cache of elk meat. Two disrespected women turned themselves into canyon walls impossible to climb. Everything, even a mere pebble, was thought to have power—power an individual could not utilize unless he or she had a special relationship with the pebble. Violation of any aspect of the natural world—people included—would be punished, in some cases even by death. As I mentioned earlier, physical violence was considered the lowest form of warfare; if you struck a person, you only demonstrated to others you had no spiritual power. Cutting down a tree was also considered a violent act. Early ethnographers characterized our culture as being predicated on black magic and fear; but might we not see it for what it was: predicated on profound respect and a fundamental belief that no one of us is the center of the universe? Doesn't this humility help explain how so many people living so close together and speaking so many different languages maintained for so long their sustainable relationships with both one another and the land?

When white people came to the area, we saw how much their values differed from ours. The Kashaya Pomo word for white people is *pala-cha*, or miracles, and an elder told me the reason: When white people entered this land, they killed humans, they killed animals, and they chopped down trees, but instead of getting punished, instead of this violence turning back on them, more white people arrived and the violence continued. We thought they were miraculous. Those ancestors who first encountered Europeans, if only they could see the world today. Not so miraculous, after all. The same elder prophesied that one day white people would come to us to "learn our ways in order to save the earth and all living things. They will want to know [because] they will want to help. I think that day is here. You young people must not forget the things us old ones is telling you."

When we went into the redwoods, we did so with purpose. We gathered huckleberries and ferns from clearings inside the forest; mushrooms and clover, too. We snared rabbits in nets beneath huckleberry bramble. Known routes through the trees connected inland valleys and plains to the ocean, and we used them with caution. Certain people had greater knowledge of the redwoods than others and therefore took more liberties. Human Bears, for instance—individuals who, having been carefully selected and secretly trained by elder cult members, donned grizzly bear hides, and were endowed with the strength of the bear—traveled great distances at night through the trees, but even they were careful. There was much to be wary of. There was a tribe of Little People in the forest, humans only two feet tall, rarely amicable, easily irritated. Slug Woman lived in the forest, too. At night, near the edge of the woods, you might hear the tinkling of abalone pendants attached to the empty baby cradle she carries or, worse, you might catch sight of the glistening shells. Don't follow, lest she lead you into the trees, only to return you with no memory.

The Little People and Slug Woman have been in the

redwood forests a long time. Coyote planted them there when he created the world from the top of Sonoma Mountain with the assistance of his nephew Chicken Hawk. At that time, all of the animals and birds and plants and trees were people. Redwood trees were old people in Coyote's village. They were wise because they were the oldest. It is said that when they took the form of trees they made themselves the color of blood because they wanted to remind us that we are all the same, that we were all people once from the same village on Sonoma Mountain. They went west and grew tall so we could see them and their red color and remember the story.

Growing up, I never thought much about redwood trees. They were there, like oak trees, like Santa Rosa Creek, like cars, like Jersey and Holstein cows in the fields outside of town. I worked on dairies as a small kid, and once, searching for a lost heifer—I must've been six or seven—I wandered into a grove of redwoods. Looking back, the trees must've been relatively young, but I remember now how quickly the forest became dark, and then how I'd found the heifer, with buzzards perched on her bloated body and stiff legs, halted in their feeding to look at me.

I didn't think of redwood trees when the old man offered

me his charmstone. If he was going to mention redwood pitch, I never gave him the chance. He called me from the street as I was making my way to my friend's house around the corner, and though I was only fifteen years old, I should've known better than to approach him. The unshaven, crotchety old codger sold heroin, and we'd seen twenty-year-old girls, presumably addicts, traipse in and out of his house. Sitting in the shade of his front porch, he said to me something along the lines of what he might've said to any potential initiate: "You'll be able to get anyone you want with this stone." I felt, looking at the oblong object in his hand, as if he were asking me to fondle him.

I didn't know then that I was Indian, but I'd heard Indian stories, and even witnessed some of the unbelievable things described in them. My friends—the same ones who lived around the corner from the old man—had a great-uncle who, they said, could turn into a hummingbird and travel at great speed. He was the same man who'd spooked Mabel and Essie while they sipped a soda in Thrifty's. Again, he was a large man, heavyset, and he wore a fedora and, even on warm days, a thick overcoat. One day, as a gaggle of us teenagers piled into a car, he waved at us from the front door. Five minutes later, we were stopped at a red light uptown and there he was, waving from a park bench. Strange—like so many of the Indian stories I'd heard. When the old man offered me the charm-stone, I didn't think of him as being someone like my friends' great-uncle, someone who might have had ancient knowledge or powers. He didn't seem like anyone in the stories I'd heard. I tried to forget about him.

Mabel McKay was the first person I told about the encoun-ter. When the memory surfaced, she was telling me stories for the book I was helping her write. (I'd known her son Marshall since junior high school, but little did I know then that his mother was a renowned Pomo medicine woman and basket weaver, or that twenty years later I would write a book about her life, *Weaving the Dream* (1994)). It was late, near mid-night, and she'd been talking for hours. She didn't like the tape recorder; she wanted me to listen. She mentioned some-thing about a Mexican Indian shaman she'd met recently, and when she fished a glassy quartz crystal from under a clutter of coiled sedge roots and redbud bark that she used for basket making and then pushed the crystal across her kitchen table to me, I not only regained my focus but instantly thought of the charmstone in the old man's open palm. I told her what I could remember from twenty years before, describing the stone and what the man had said. Given his age at the time of our encounter, I was certain he had died by then. Mabel, however, talked to me—warned me—as if his offer still stood.

"Here's the deal," she began. "Them poisons is old—that kind of poison to get people you want, it's old. That's why they use ancient things to put in it. But here's the deal: Once you agree to use the poison, you have to agree not to forget. Sometimes you can sell it to people. But, no matter what, a person can't die until he passes it on to someone else. That's the rule."

"So he was offering me love medicine," I said. "Maybe he wanted to die."

"I don't know," Mabel said after a minute.

She told me she knew the man. She told me that she'd heard he'd killed his first wife, that he'd drowned her in Tomales Bay. I recognized the woman's name—she was my grandmother's cousin.

"You see," Mabel said, "here's the other thing: Yes, you can get anyone you want, but then you are stuck with them for everlasting. That's the power of the ingredients. Yeah, they use sap from the redwood trees. It makes the memory stick . . . I don't do them things, but that's what I heard."

Mabel sat back in her chair. She adjusted her modish glasses and looked at me. Then she started chuckling. "You don't need it," she said. "Try the regular way. You're good-looking enough."

She leaned forward and picked up the crystal, displaying it in her open hand.

"Why did that Mexican Indian doctor give that to you?" I asked. "What's it for?"

She laughed out loud, uproariously. Then she stopped. With the crystal still in her hand, and just before she burst out laughing again, she said, "It's to keep you awake. You was falling asleep."

So I knew. When the woman with the love medicine made her offer and told me its ingredients and chanted its song, I knew what she wasn't telling me, the commitment I'd have no choice but to keep if I were to accept her offer. I'd heard the stories about her, yes; but I figured that with what I knew—and what I wasn't telling her I knew—I could keep one step ahead of her. She'd asked me to her cottage outside of Sebastopol, saying she was concerned about how elders had been treated at the Indian Health Clinic. While she was not enrolled in my tribe, she was a relative and I felt compelled to hear her out. She'd finished talking about her unfaithful husband and her old aunt's offer, which I assumed she'd accepted, and I was expecting to hear about the two of them going to the redwoods where it is dark at noon, but instead she began chanting, and in English of all things.

Your name is on my lips
Your name is on my lips
Your name is on my lips
Your name is on my lips

Your name is on my lips
Your name is on my lips
Your name is on my lips
Your name is on my lips

"That's the song my old aunt taught me. She said, 'You have to hear it first.'"

Okay, I thought. She's trying to trap me, singing the song, thinking she's caught me off guard. But why in English? Did the song work the same in English? And why me? Mabel told me anyone with powers to pass on—and especially poisoners—often look for a certain kind of person. They want the lonely and scared people who need to attach themselves to something in this world. At the time I had encountered the old man and his stone, I was more or less lost. I didn't know who my father was. I didn't know I was Coast Miwok and Pomo. But now I was chairman of my tribe, the Federated Indians of Graton Rancheria. I had power and influence. Wasn't that why this woman had invited me to her house in the first place?

"So what happened at the clinic?" I asked quickly, changing the subject.

I'd interrupted her and, easily enough, she'd lost her train of thought and launched into how difficult it was to make an appointment at the clinic, how rude the operators had been to the elders.

I felt rude myself then. I should've at least asked her about the song, about how it sounded in Pomo. I understood some Pomo. I could have let her talk. But then no, what was I thinking? I'd only encourage her. Perhaps she was sick. Perhaps she was going to die. Was that why she was trying to pass on her love medicine to me? She was not too old—fiftyish, spry, it seemed. Her shock of graying hair was cut stylishly at her ears. Her color was good, her eyes shone. She moved in her chair with ease. Did she want to tell me she needed extra attention at the clinic on account of some undisclosed disease she'd been diagnosed with?

"And listen to this," she quipped. "A woman—a friend of mine—made an appointment and when she go to the clinic, they didn't even have it written down, and they were rude to her, making her feel like she was crazy, like she had Alzheimer's disease. It's not for me, you know. I'm fine. I'm concerned about the old people. They wanted me to talk to you," she finished, dispelling my theories about her health.

But if she had wanted to talk to me about the clinic, how in the world had we gotten on the topic of love medicine? Had it been related to her telling me about an elder shortly after I'd sat down with her? I couldn't remember. I hadn't been paying close enough attention. Feeling generous, I turned the conversation back around. I figured I'd get her to the end of her story and then be done with it.

"So did it work, the love medicine? Did you get your husband back?"

"Oh," she laughed, as if she too had just remembered what we'd been talking about. "Listen, that fool started showing up everywhere. He'd come to my back door at night and cry, 'Please take me back. Please, my sweetheart.' Ha! One time I was at the movies downtown and I turned around and found him in the seat behind me. What did I do right in the middle of the movie? I bent over and said out loud, 'Kiss my ass.'"

I laughed. Then she picked up the story where she'd first left off.

"So I went there, to the redwoods, with my aunt. They was

big trees, all right." She paused, then looked away from me to the window before saying what I took as a blatant offer. "They're there yet, them big trees. There's big trees yet by the Russian River."

When she said no more, I started talking again about potential changes to the health clinic's governing board and how that might help the situation there, and before I left, she thanked me for taking the time to hear her concerns. "The old people will be happy," she said. At the door, smiling, she thanked me again.

Later that afternoon, after reporting the woman's concerns to the health clinic, I drove to Wohler Bridge on the Russian River. Across the bridge, on the north side of the water, is a stand of redwoods, certainly not first- or second-growth trees, but tall enough. These were the trees that had come to mind when the woman mentioned redwoods and the Russian River. The water was clear and shallow enough for a person to wade to the trees on the other side. The trees looked dark, a wall of trunks and thick foliage on the riverbanks. The temperature inside the stand felt cool, even cold at times, no matter how warm the summer day. Once, a friend, barefoot and naked in the trees, undoubtedly either not knowing or not thinking about my heritage, said, "Wow! This must've been what it was like being an Indian around here." I might've laughed and asked for whatever it was he was smoking. I didn't tell him what crossed my mind, what I thought about the place just a stone's throw from the beach, where the old folks gathered herbs for colds and asthma. Or how half a mile north of the beach a jealous man murdered my grandmother's cousin and left her under a thicket of willow. Or how first-generation Filipino men fought roosters under the bridge.

Much has changed here. The river is deep and still in the summer. The water, a putrid green, is unhealthy. "No Trespassing" signs line property on both banks. But the trees are still there. The county maintains a small regional park and has placed picnic tables under the redwoods and provided a lot where seasonal visitors pay a fee for parking. Seated at a table, I let my mind wander. Had I always been able to hear cars passing over the bridge? I couldn't remember being able to see the river from inside the trees, like I could now. What had changed? Was it the park visitors—now a couple walking their dog—that distracted me?

Memories appeared and fled. I thought of looking for pitch, maybe on one of the tree trunks or perhaps oozing from a broken branch; the woman hadn't said where to look. Her babbling about love medicine felt remote now. Why had I taken time to come here? Any sense of urgency that I'd felt hearing her talk, and even the sense of urgency and awe these trees might inspire, escaped me. This grove couldn't have been where she'd come with her aunt to learn about love medicine.

I walked to the road and onto the bridge, where I could look down on the dirty water. I remembered the warm sand, the shallow, clear river. Talk of redwood trees and the river reminded me of those carefree days. I watched a pair of sparrows dart back and forth above the water. I didn't see an osprey, but maybe I just hadn't waited long enough.

Prior to the gold rush era, the coast redwoods covered a range of two million acres. Today, only 5 percent of those ancient forests remain. Extensive logging of redwoods began in 1850, and mills soon sprung up throughout the region, located near railroads and waterways built to facilitate transportation of the wood to burgeoning San Francisco. In the 1840s, Stephen Smith, a sea captain and entrepreneur from Boston, had opened the first steam-generated mill in the town of Bodega, where, after marrying fifteen-year-old Peruvian Manuela Torres for the purpose of obtaining a Mexican land grant, he fathered three legitimate children as well as several more with his maid, a Coast Miwok woman named Tsupu and baptized Maria Checca, my great-great-great-grandmother.

As the redwoods suffered and fell, so did the indigenous people. In 1850, vagrancy laws and indentured servitude, both utilized by the Mexican rancheros, were incorporated into the Act for the Government and Protection of Indians, the act that legalized Indian slavery and remained in full effect until 1868, three years after the end of the Civil War. According to the law of the land, stealing a white man's Indian was tantamount to stealing his horse.

Spanish laws imposed on Natives sought not only to restrict their freedom and their use of the land (as with the prohibition on controlled burning) but also to take power over how they managed themselves. One rule said Natives could not bathe at will in the missions; offended by their nudity, the Spanish padres permitted only an occasional bath with a bucket of water. Our people, cloaked in European clothes and unable to sweat and bathe in the traditional ways, became even more susceptible to European diseases to which we had no immunity, and pneumonia, smallpox, and syphilis ravaged mission populations and spread to unconquered villages. Conservative estimates suggest twenty thousand Coast Miwok and Southern Pomo inhabited present-day Marin County and the southern part of Sonoma County at the time of European contact. Today, more than two centuries later, of the fourteen hundred enrolled members of the Federated Indians of Graton Rancheria, all descend from one of fourteen survivors from the original population. The survival rate was then, and is still, lower than that of the ancient redwoods, which also suffered at the hands of these same people.

As the trees disappeared, so did the forests' flora and fauna. Without cover of the dark woods, the most powerful creatures of the land, the grizzly bears, were vulnerable to farmers anxious to kill them to protect their livestock. Vaquero culture, which grew out of the Mexican rancho period, made sport of killing the huge creatures, lassoing them from horseback before shooting them, and many Americans adopted this practice. Arenas were built wherein, for the entertainment of settlers, captured bears were pitted against longhorn bulls in a fight to the death. The arenas' fences were made of the most durable lumber—redwood.

In the absence of redwood shade, mushrooms and mosses, exposed to direct sun, dried up, and redwood sorrel and redwood orchids, trillium and fairy bells, disappeared. Native foods such as huckleberries and several varieties of clover, also dependent on the forests' shade, became harder to find.

Acorns, a staple of the California Indian diet, were also endangered, as tanoaks, on which grow the acorns most suitable for mush and bread, were no longer able to thrive in redwood clearings. The loss of tanoak groves also put the remaining redwoods in danger, as the smaller trees serve as buffers against fierce coastal winds and rains that can fell the towering giants; redwoods have a shallow root system and no taproot to anchor them, and the most frequent cause of death, next to logging, is windthrow. Salmon, another principal food source, and an important part of the larger ecosystem, have also been affected by threats to the redwoods. When the land is in balance, fish spawn in streams that flow uninterrupted under the trees, and when the fish die after spawning, their decaying bodies provide important nutrients to the trees. When the trees are cut, this cycle is broken. Sediment from logged hillsides clog the streams, and succeeding generations of salmon cannot navigate their way to spawn. The fish disappear. The people don't eat. Second-growth trees don't eat.

In the face of these changes, surviving Natives adopted the settlers' diet. We learned to eat wheat and corn. With game scarce, we ate beef. What we wanted to do but couldn't was put things back in place. We couldn't open the grasslands for elk and pronghorn. We couldn't unclog the streams. The sedge beds where our mothers and grandmothers had gathered roots for basket making, where were they? Where was the lake full of perch and catfish? Where did the redwoods go? Increasingly, we became strangers in our homeland. What happened to the outcropping of rocks that told the story of the greedy hunter? Isn't that wheat field where my grandfather's village was? No wonder the white man's religion began to make sense to some of us. Home isn't here, it's in the sky someplace.

The North Bay fire did not reach my home on Sonoma Mountain, but it came close. Driving down the mountain, after my neighbor's desperate 2 a.m. call to evacuate, I saw in the otherwise black night towering flames fifty feet from my car and, looking north to Santa Rosa, endless flames into the distance, an apocalyptic inferno. On the east side of the mountain, above the town of Glen Ellen, young, hand-planted redwood trees burned along with other trees caught in the fire. Within the last fifty years, developers have lined neighborhood thoroughfares and freeways with redwood trees, and homeowners have planted them in their backyards. Without the support of ancient giants that would, in a natural setting, grow alongside them, however, and without the requisite amount of fog that supplies 40 percent of a coast redwood's moisture, it remains to be seen if these inland trees will reach adulthood. (And that's not to mention what will happen if climate change affects the amount of fog redwoods will receive even when growing in their current range.) Can a young redwood tree withstand fire the way an older one can? A redwood's life span is two thousand years. A fifty-year-old tree is an infant.

The oldest redwood trees in Sonoma County live in Armstrong Redwoods State Natural Reserve. One tree is fourteen hundred years old, another 310 feet high. Today the eight-hundred-acre reserve features picnic facilities, an outdoor amphitheater, and self-guided nature trails, but the main attraction is the ancient redwood grove, which the park's webpage notes is "a living reminder of the magnificent primeval redwood forest that covered much of this area before logging operations began during the nineteenth century." According to the website, "Colonel James Armstrong, an early-day lumberman, recognized the beauty and natural value of the forests he harvested [and] set aside the area as a 'natural park and botanical garden.'" But of course he hadn't "discovered" this natural wonder; local Natives had lived beside it for centuries. Why hadn't I thought of *these* trees when I was told about love medicine?

Not long after the fire, I drove to Armstrong State Reserve, just outside of Guerneville, on the Russian River. More and more, I'd been thinking about love medicine, of the woman's mention of pitch from old trees. I wasn't interested in collecting the sap, or even seeing it—that is, if I was even able to find it. And anyway, I never did hear about the other necessary ingredients for the love medicine, and I'd long ago heeded Mabel McKay's advice to go about romance "the regular way." The main things on my mind were the recent fires and, to be honest, completing this essay. I had to write something. Go look at old redwoods, I told myself.

It was late afternoon when I arrived, the autumn sun already low in the sky, the day still unseasonably warm. From the parking lot, the trees were magnificent indeed, towering above the blacktop and cars. Each trunk was the size of a dozen people huddled together. Wisps of poison ivy lined a path to the picnic tables, the autumn-red leaves like lights announcing the forest.

Inside the forest, seated at a picnic table, I watched as the narrow columns of light filtering through the trees changed color, orange to red-violet. I thought of the things I knew. Was I seeing in that interplay of light and forest a thread for my imagination? The darkening light had to be the color of redwood pitch. Here, in these trees, the last Pomo woman who knew the ingredients and song for love medicine had walked with her old aunt for the first time. Kiss my ass. Isn't that what she'd said to the husband who'd jilted her? When the whale was at the mouth of the Gualala River, did water cover the forest here? The sharp scent of redwoods, pungent in the warm air, reminded me of sand beside a clean river. As daylight waned, the trees seemed to grow taller. I wanted to feel myself grow even smaller beneath them. But that didn't happen. I contented myself with what I'd seen earlier in that interplay of light and forest, that long play of history, the interrelatedness of all things, what I had understood in a single color—the color of pitch from a redwood tree. I saw my place in that history. And there was one thing more.

Days later the weather changed. Fog returned. My house sits high enough on Sonoma Mountain so that, looking west from my kitchen window, I can see the fog covering the Santa Rosa plain to form an inland sea. On that morning, I could see the tops of the trees on the coastal hills poking above the fog. That is how the trees must've looked as my ancestors watched the ocean recede. And then the woman was there, above the fog and smiling confidently, just as she had when she'd said goodbye to me from her front door, only now she was saying hello. I understood. She never taught me love medicine.

Maybe never cared to.

What she did do for me was enough. The trees. I couldn't forget.

IF OPRAH WERE AN OAK TREE

I am learning about "sudden oak death." Specifically, I am learning to see it outside my window: I understand that the crimson-colored bleeding canker on the trunk of the magnificent three-hundred-year-old live oak in the middle of my garden indicates lethal infection, presages the tree's imminent death.

My first thoughts are selfish: I will have to cut down the tree. That is, I will have to pay someone to cut down the tree, otherwise risk an enormous corpse crashing atop my kitchen. Below my yard, bordering my neighbor's property, a live oak, equal in size and splendor to this one, died last summer, costing nearly two thousand dollars to cut down. I shared the cost with my neighbor. I will have to foot this bill alone.

Then there is the aesthetic concern, also selfish, I suppose. My home, whose modern architecture was crafted around these Sonoma Mountain ancients, which were expected to outlive the home's residents, if not the house itself, will look completely different without them.

The home's rectangular structure, meant to look integrated with the forested landscape, will appear instead an obtrusive brown box of metal and glass plunked against a naked hillside. The native ferns and grasses, dependent on the tree's shade and acidity, will give way to non-native species, including, for example, the oatgrass and numerous varieties of thistle that commonly flourish on the dry, open hillside here.

All of the live oaks around my home—indeed in the entire region—show signs of infection, if only foliar lesions, the first, and omnipresent, indication of the disease's presence. In any given stand of infected live oaks the mortality rate is presently 40 to 80 percent. Will I have two trees left? One?

The history of sudden oak death (SOD), and the scientific community's frustration with it, not to mention the ongoing devastation, sounds a lot like the AIDS story.

In May 1997, Marin County homeowners noticed live oaks beginning to die in their gardens. Two years earlier, in April 1995, the UC Cooperative Extension office in Marin had been asked to investigate an unusual dieback of more than a dozen tanoaks bordering a creek, and in June "a shocking number" of dead trees, described by Pavel Svihra in his case study of SOD, was noted on the slope above the creek and along the crest of the hill. The dying live oaks, reported in 1997, showed symptoms similar to those of these tanoaks, and scientists suspected the same causes—prolonged drought from 1990 to 1992 followed by very wet years in 1993 and 1994, which might have reduced the trees' vigor, making them susceptible to infestations of various fungi and bark beetles, none of which normally kill healthy trees.

In June 1998, the word "epidemic" was used—live oaks, tanoaks, and now black oaks were dying from Mill Valley to Novato. By 1999 tens of thousands of trees in Marin and Sonoma Counties were infected. By the year 2000, when David Rizzo, a UC professor, isolated the pathogen now believed to be the primary causal agent of SOD—a heretofore unknown fungus of the *Phytophthora* genus, termed a year later *Phytophthora ramorum*—the disease was present in twelve California counties, most notably in Marin, Santa Cruz, and Sonoma. Today it is found in an additional thirteen species from ten plant families that act as hosts—redwoods and rhododendrons among them. So far, the disease appears fatal only to the three oak species—live oaks, tanoaks, black oaks. Yet as Pavel Svihra notes, "There are no measures available that will alter the underlying disease [*P. ramorum*]."

My Coast Miwok ancestors depended on oak trees. Acorns were for us, and for all central California tribes, what rice has been for China and wheat for Europe. For ages, acorns fed some of the densest precontact populations in the New World. Acorns from live oaks proved the most difficult to harvest and store, and yielded a meal, or mush, that was greasy, though good for making bread.

Tanoaks provided the acorns of choice. Coast Miwok and Southern Pomo located inland traded with those on the coast for access to the trees. The tanoaks have been the hardest hit by SOD, with 90 percent of the stands in many areas decimated. The moist coastal climate, which the tanoaks prefer, affords, unfortunately, the best condition for the reproduction of the pathogen *P. ramorum* and its spread to the trees, which our northwestern neighbors, the Kashaya Pomo, simply called *cisq qhale*, beautiful tree.

My home sits less than a quarter-mile from the site of the Alaguali village. Friends' ancestors come from Alaguali. (My ancestors hail from nearby Petaluma and Bodega Bay.) I imagine these ancestors, women with tattooed chins, men sporting seal bone nose plugs and finely chipped abalone pendant earrings, raking with hand-crafted wooden instruments the old leaves and worm-infested acorns from under the tree outside my window, halting the spread of worm and other parasite infections that would tax the health of this wondrous individual. With obsidian-bladed knives they cut suckers around the tree's base and on its gnarled trunk. Every five to ten years they set fire to the area, burning undergrowth that would sap nutrients from the soil, and at the same time replenishing the ground with ash, which the tree desperately needs and depends on. That was about two hundred years ago, when the tree was one hundred.

Then the Europeans—the tree witnessed the first Spanish livestock, herds of curly-horned cattle and spotted horses that roamed into these hills from the mission plantation in Sonoma and from as far away as the mission in San Rafael. These animals carried foreign seed in their dung: oatgrass, mustard, and thistle replaced peppergrass and showy clover on the sunny slope beyond the tree's canopy. And, as I mentioned before, the padres imposed—and were insistent upon—a ban against controlled burning, as they wanted the grass for their livestock, and at the same time they also ordered a ban against bathing. Did the dense clusters of pinprick leaves register a pneumonic cough, perhaps feel the heat of a human's death—presaging fever?

General Vallejo and his army of Mexican soldiers who secularized the missions and established the extensive ranchos intensified the simultaneous destruction of Coast Miwok lifeways and the aboriginal landscape. Among other disruptive acts, the American settler named William Bihler bombed with dynamite the southern end of Tolay Lake, a sacred place for the Coast Miwok, draining the lake of water, rendering a dried lake bed suitable for planting wheat and corn. Certainly the earth trembled with the blasts. Blasts, blasts, blasts . . . This tree outside my window felt all of them, shuddered, with dynamite and gun blasts alike, dynamite imploding entire hills, blasting enormous crater-like holes in the mountain, gun blasts dropping the last elk, pronghorn, grizzly bear and black bear; shovels, then drills, digging into the earth for water; thudding tractors, more dynamite, carving up the mountainside, flattening ridges for roads, then paving the roads; oh, and lest I forget, no doubt an enormous steel crane, an unearthly monster, driving piles into the ground for the foundation of this house!

I marvel at the history I imagine recorded in the tree's life. I think of a young couple taken from Alaguali, my friends' ancestors, baptized by the Spanish padres as Isidro and Isidra. Did they miss the tree? Enslaved at the San Rafael mission, did Isidro and Isidra look up one late autumn afternoon, him tending cattle, her ironing the padres' vestments, and wonder if there was anyone still who might rake the leaves and wormy acorns from under the tree? Did the tree miss their songs, and the click and the *sh* in the words of their conversations? Does it understand Spanish or English? This tree and its ancestors for ten thousand years heard only Coast Miwok and Pomo languages from humans. Forget ten thousand years, think time immemorial for my people.

Once, Indians on foot came up and down this spirit- and oak-filled mountain, and now I, an Indian tribal chairman, come up and down the mountain at least once a day in a car (never mind that it's a Prius), along with a couple hundred other people, all of them up and down the mountain in their cars, too. This heady notion of history I glean from the tree's point of view—a lofty vision of time—distracts me from my baser preoccupations with money and aesthetics regarding the tree's impending demise. Even as I implicate myself—my home, my driving up and down the mountain—as part of a story that hasn't related a necessarily pleasant experience for the tree, I congratulate myself for knowing as much . . . that is, until I recall what a short chapter of the tree's history I have a sense of.

Time immemorial? The oak trees, along with their bay laurel neighbors, have been here forty million years.

I remember being startled by screaming—cheering?—coming from the TV set. It was Oprah, or rather, her audience. Oprah was giving each of her perfectly coifed, perfectly thirtysomething guests one of her "favorite things." In this case it was a kitchen utensil. What, a blender? A juicer? As if she had spent a lot of time in her local appliance store, or even her kitchen, testing such things.

Okay, I admit it. I was watching *Oprah*. At one o'clock in the morning, after a long day of writing, teaching, and overseeing the daily operations of my tribe, I turned on the TV, mostly to see the news, but flicking the channels I found, or landed on, *Oprah*, a repeat from a 4:00 p.m. broadcast a decade ago. She still fascinates us. Why is everyone hooked on Oprah?

We care about her "favorite things"—foods, clothes, vacation spots, furniture, kitchen appliances, books, cars, celebrities, you name it. We care about what her interior designer can tell us about chintz and color schemes, and what her makeup artist can tell us about lip gloss and face creams. We care what her psychologist says about our problems. Did we know we had such problems? And of course we care about what her favorite poet, Maya Angelou, says about our souls. We care about Oprah. Who doesn't know the story of the poor girl from Mississippi who became the most powerful woman in show business? Doesn't her story prove that all of us can overcome personal obstacles? We care about her weight issues. We care about her daily life. Have you called the number where you can listen to "private conversations" between her and her best friend Gayle? Oprah's social and political causes become our own. Have you donated to Oprah's Angel Network? Her heroes become our heroes. For example, the young girl (on the repeat show two nights ago), who saved her mother from a bear attack in her living room, and the fireman in Hawaii who saved a girl after her car had plunged into the ocean and was five feet under water. Real life stuff, fantastic or ordinary, we watch it on *Oprah*. And if you miss Oprah on TV, perhaps because you don't watch TV, you will see her in the supermarket. Whole Foods or Safeway, doesn't matter. Her O *Magazine* is prominently displayed alongside *People* and *Star*. It's always Oprah on the cover, because, as her best friend Gayle once said, "People want to see Oprah." Is it possible to *not* see Oprah?

I rushed to the TV to see what Oprah was giving away.

Toothpaste coating my mouth, eyes frozen on the screen, I no doubt resembled a rabid animal. Too late; Oprah, happy as a lark, had already moved on and was cooking something with a special guest chef. Would each of her audience members get a frying pan? Frustrated—both for missing what it was she gave away and for caring—I flicked off the TV.

Later, I heard the tree scraping against the house. Wind; I would have to sweep leaves in the morning, a chore compulsive sorts like myself don't like to think about before bed. Then a second thought: before long there would be no leaves to sweep.

Is there any chance the tree will survive? Can we find a cure? Could Oprah help?

Better yet, what if Oprah were an oak tree? The oak tree outside my window, for instance.

Each weekday, Monday through Friday, promptly at 4:00 p.m. on CBS, you would see on *The Live Oak Show* the tree outside my window. Featured in the middle of your screen would be the oak tree, long shots, close-ups, and numerous profile shots, the camera cutting back and forth from the tree to its various guests, the vast majority human, most of whom would be talking about the tree. Of course there would be shows that featured psychics, mediums who claim to channel the spirits of the trees, who would talk on camera *with* the tree. As certain guests discussed the tree's physical properties, the camera would pan from the gnarled trunk, properly called a bole, as the audience would be informed, to the myriad branches and onto the curled prickly leaves. During a special fall-season show featuring acorn harvesting techniques, the camera would zoom in on hands collecting nuts off the ground and, later on the same show, provide close-ups on proper rakes and techniques for clearing away from under the tree the old leaves and the wormy nuts that had been left behind during the collecting phase. That show would end with a tight low-angle shot of the pile of debris burning—a voice-over reminding us that ash is good for the tree.

The programs that cause the most angst in viewers (even as they are the programs with the highest ratings) have to do with the tree's health status. Mid-season, during a program on foliar lesions, the frame would zoom in on numerous leaf samples, and special cameras would catch microscopic cellular activity, including the presence, or not, of that life-threatening pathogen *P. ramorum*. The next season would premiere with a shot of the bleeding canker, a painful sight no one can forget—viewer discretion advised—an image that keeps viewers hooked the entire season. Will we get to see the canker again?

When? Will it be worse? Better?

There would be a show about the tree's "favorite things": ash and other nutrients that enhance its ability to fight disease; methods of pruning that enhance its beauty and overall vitality, using (of course) its favorite shears, modeled after indigenous tools that prove the least painful or disturbing to the tree; birds—chickadees during the winter months, and sapsuckers, finches, and sparrows during spring and summer, with flickers, jays, and pileated woodpeckers in the fall—all of which help control parasites harmful to the tree; acid-loving flora, ferns, and such on the ground below the tree; native grasses and bulbs beyond the tree's canopy (peppergrass, various clovers, bluedicks, and poppies that maintain the local terrain by assuring, among other things, adequate water retention); rain free of acid; air free of pollutants; stable weather patterns.

One show would be devoted entirely to scientific research on SOD. We would learn about whatever progress is being made on the disease, new discoveries about its life cycle and methods of transmission, and there would be an Angel Network of sorts, let's call it the Oak Tree Spirit Network, that we could donate to for further research. Another show would feature the tree's cousins, its immediate live oak neighbors, as well as its distant relatives, black oaks and white oaks, the latter, interestingly enough, *not* killed by SOD. Tanoaks, which live farthest from the tree—rarely, if ever, on Sonoma Mountain, but west, along the coast—are also the most distantly related of its oak relatives.

A series of shows lasting an entire week would follow a team comprised of scientists, politicians, and Coast Miwok and Southern Pomo descendants as they journey up the mountain on foot to the tree. Scientists would point out copses of live oaks, noting infection rates as well as native and non-native plant and animal species and the likely impact of climate change on the ecology of the region. Politicians would take notes, commit to more funding for research on SOD and on climate control, understanding that a warmer climate challenges the well-being not only of the ancient oaks—in particular the tree outside my window—but of all life as we know it on Sonoma Mountain. After all, climate change creates conditions for new pathogens like *P. ramorum*. The Coast Miwok and Southern Pomo descendants would repeat the ancient adage that people cannot forget the tree lest the trees forget the people, and, once the party reaches the tree, these aboriginal descendants would speak to the tree in their revitalized native languages. A fire is burned under the tree, mimicking old controlled-burning practices, as an offering to the tree, and the scientists point out that temperatures above 95 degrees Fahrenheit kill *P. ramorum*. Finally, everyone enjoys a taste of mush or bread made from the tree's acorns. It is a cannot-miss *Live Oak Show* week.

On the cover of each *O Magazine*—that is, the oak magazine—would be a flattering picture of the tree: in spring, the tree against a landscape lush green with assorted golden poppies and purple lupine; in summer, the tree, stately, against the warm, sun-dried slopes; in fall, with Native baskets, used for harvesting, at its base, the rich designs and earth tones of the baskets complimenting the tree's colors and textures; in winter, the tree glistening wet, ferns, glistening likewise, below it.

Saturday Night Live would make fun of the oak tree, with skits imitating various memorable episodes, like the one that featured Brad Pitt and Angelina Jolie talking about the seedlings they adopted. Social critics would point out that many of *The Live Oak Show*'s sponsors were not fully politically correct in terms of fair trade and labor practices, not to mention the toll the magazine's enormous subscription rate takes on the forests in Canada and South America, and the outcry would prompt the sponsors to clean up their act, and the magazine itself would convert to being published solely on recycled paper.

Thinking critically about its popularity, the show would feature a program exploring the tree's celebrity. What makes the tree so popular? Why are we hooked on that specific tree outside my window? The most simple and obvious explanation, used by psychologists, is that the media, and specifically its ability to mass-produce images of the tree, forces us to become familiar with it. It becomes commonplace, as well known as a member of our immediate family. We see it as often as the people we live with, and, if we pay attention—that is, if we watch the television show with even a modicum of ardor or regularly read the magazine—we may know more about the history and daily life of the tree than of the people in our own households. Or at least we think we do. Other psychologists and media experts would point out the irony that the tree's celebrity is simultaneously based on, and maintained by, the fact that it is on TV, and that, in fact, we don't know it at all, or only to the extent producers and such want us to know it. Bottom line: The tree outside my window *can't* be likened to the tree outside your window, for then it would become truly commonplace and no longer of such intense fascination.

The irony, understood by anyone with an interest in the workings of mass media, seems symptomatic of the larger culture and history of which it is part. In an ironic yet very noticeable way, we don't *know* our own homes. We may occupy our homes, our neighborhoods, our bioregions, our watersheds, whatever, but we are simultaneously separated from them, not engaged with them. Thus, we are strangers where we live. We are here but not here, home but not home. At some point, all of us, Native and non-Native, developed, or perhaps accepted as a result of military defeat and colonization, a culture characterized by this condition. Aboriginal people—let's start with the Israelites—were removed from their native land, or home, and enslaved and then freed, finding themselves in a place with only a *promise* of land, or home, once again. This story has played itself out multiple times, replicating a pattern that has disengaged so many people from their native homes that now the vast majority of the human population finds itself in this condition. Certainly, there are variations in the story, and different Native people cling to land-based lifestyles and traditions with varying degrees of success. But, for the most part, we have effectively become strangers where we live, at least from an aboriginal land-based point of view. We may no longer look specifically for a promised land, with or without our tribe, but the act of looking for home—call it security, if you wish—is the same. We set our gaze elsewhere. We think more money, a bigger house, more cattle, a script that will sell, whatever it may be, will get us *there*. Often governments and historical circumstances provide no alternatives, if they even allow us opportunity to pursue such things, but the trick—and the truth—is that as long as we remain separated from our home, not fully engaged with it, looking elsewhere, we will always be insecure. It will feel natural to see, perhaps dream, of home and security down the road, next year, in another life. It will feel natural to look at the tree on TV and not at the one outside your window. The tree on TV will be real to us. We've learned to look that way.

Could *The Live Oak Show* be popular because environmentalism is popular? I'd like to imagine so. But to what extent, then, does environmentalism remain an idea and not something lived? The tree's survival, not to mention our own as a species, depends on our living connectedness with the world, and most importantly with the local world, our home. The danger of seeing only the celebrity tree is not only that we don't see the tree outside our window but that we don't see our relationship to that tree, how our lives, and the decisions we make, impact its well-being. A celebrity culture—let's say any culture disengaged from its home—is in many ways a blind culture. If we don't see the tree outside our window, if we are not truly at home in our home, how can we understand our connection with it? How can we know to be responsible? This blindness, in fact, helps maintain the disconnection that maintains, in turn, the blindness—a very dark circle, a patch over our eyes.

Looking at the tree outside my window offers vision. It suggests a history I am implicated in and inextricable from, not just in terms of my Coast Miwok ancestors but *now*, while the tree and I are alive in the same home. My car trips up and down the mountain contribute to poor air quality, as does anything I purchase in the grocery store or local mall that requires the burning of fossil fuels, whether strawberries from Watsonville 120 miles away or a pair of tennis shoes made in China. What I plant under the tree, or near it, and the amount of water those plants require—these things also affect the tree's well-being, as do the types of fertilizers I use. My neighbors, too: whatever they plant, whatever livestock and pets they own, affect the tree. The Angus cattle in the nearby hills continue to spread exotic seed. Sulfites used in the non-organic grape vineyard down the road waft in the air and poison the groundwater.

Domestic cats—two live next door—kill birds that clean the tree of parasites. Dogs—there's an adorable yellow lab in the yard two houses down—can spread viruses that kill the native blue fox, the predator so necessary for the containment of squirrel populations. Too many squirrels deplete the tree of acorns. Never mind that without acorns the tree won't be able to produce seedlings—what if one day I needed those acorns for food?

This tree engages me with my world. Vision and connection. It's still giving, the ancient oak. I sense irony in this, and something at once sad and beautiful too, and urgent.

This morning I went out to rake leaves. The tree these days is dropping quite a few of them. The mid-April sun was warm. The gentle slopes in the distance were bright with buttercups and purple lupine. But, alas, when I turned back to the tree, bamboo rake in hand, there was the large gnarled trunk, the bleeding canker at its center, startlingly crimson in the light. I wanted to turn away, move to the other side of the tree where the canker wasn't visible. Oh, where were those yellow and purple hills? But too late. I'd seen what I'd seen. I felt depressed. My thoughts over the last few days appeared banal, plain stupid, particularly the notion of Oprah as this tree. Stupid metaphor. But this tree—the ugly canker—was important, wasn't it? Couldn't I find a more meaningful way to write about it? It was, after all, talking to all of us; it was our canary in a coal mine. Then the tree made me laugh out loud. Silly English professor, with your metaphors and meanings, good God. Canary in a coal mine? Why not the tree in front of me?

ANCESTORS

THE LAST WOMAN FROM PETALUMA

Her Indian name, or at least one of her Indian names, the only one any of us know, was Tsupu. She was my great-great-grandfather's mother, or my great-great-great-grandmother, and, again, as far as any of us know, she was the last native of Petaluma—not the city we know today but the ancient Coast Miwok village of the same name. Certainly, she was the last to pass down any memory of the place. She was quite young, perhaps fourteen, when she left, beginning what would become a chaotic, wholly incredible journey to find and keep a home in and about Sonoma County. Though the village was abandoned once and for all after the 1838 smallpox epidemic claimed its remaining citizens, and though American farmers demolished its large midden, using the centuries-old refuge of decomposed shells for fertilizer and eradicating any trace of the village, Tsupu never forgot it. The last time she visited the area she was completely blind, yet, nodding with her chin to an empty hillside, she said, "There," as if she could see her old Petaluma plain as day, tule huts and fire smoke.

The village was atop a low hill, east of the Petaluma River, located about three and a half miles northeast of the present city. Petaluma in Coast Miwok means "sloping ridge," and, as was often the custom, it was no doubt named after that distinct feature of the landscape. C. Hart Merriam, a naturalist interested in the Indians of California, wrote in 1907 that "the name Petaluma appears to have come from the Kanamara Pomo (South Pomo) on the north," but, as linguist Catherine A. Callaghan points out, Petaluma is clearly a Coast Miwok phrase. *Peta · luma*: slope ridge.

There was never a tribe or nation known as Coast Miwok; the aboriginal people of Petaluma never referred to themselves as such. Linguists and anthropologists, classifying California Natives at the turn of the twentieth century by language families, used the term Coast Miwok to describe the dozen or more distinct aboriginal nations ranging from the southern Santa Rosa plain to the northern tip of the San Francisco Bay. They were distinct from the Pomo speakers to the north and the Wappo speakers to the east. While variations among the languages of the Pomo-speaking nations were in some cases so great that different nations could not understand one another, this was not the case with Coast Miwok speakers, where variations consisted mostly in accent, as between British English and American English, and were never more diverse than Old English and Modern English, allowing Coast Miwok nations to communicate freely with one another.

Petaluma, a thriving community of at least five hundred individuals, was a major village of the Lekatuit Nation, whose territory included Petaluma Valley and extended north and west to *Potaawa · yowa*, or Chalk Ground, another large Lekatuit village, once located near the present town of Freestone. Lekatuit, which means "cross-ways willow" in Coast Miwok, was also the name of a village located just a half-mile north of the present town of Petaluma, actually closer than the aboriginal village of the same name.

The Petaluma Valley region was prized for its enormous herds of deer and elk as well as for its productive groves of valley oak and black oak. Maria Copa told anthropologist Isabel Kelly in 1932 that "deer and elk used to be plentiful in the valley this side of Petaluma [present city]—just like cattle there[, and that] Nicasio people got acorns from the Petaluma Valley." Ducks and geese flew up from the Petaluma River and its tributaries so thick as to obliterate the sun for an hour at a time, and seasonal swarms of monarch butterflies passing through the Petaluma Valley a mile wide, several miles long, forced the Lekatuit there to take refuge for sometimes a full day. Petaluma, the ancient village, was situated along a major trade route that stretched south and west through other Coast Miwok villages, and north into Pomo territory and east into Wappo and Wintun territories, and the region's abundant deer and elk and acorn supply positioned its people well to trade for what they needed from other places. More, Petaluma was considered a sacred place: On a low hill opposite the one on which the village was located, Coyote, that sometimes foolish Creator-figure for most California Indian tribes, had his conversation with Chicken Hawk about creating human beings. Again, Maria Copa said, "It was at Wotoke, a place near Petaluma, that Coyote and Walinapi [Chicken Hawk] talked first. Coyote was living on a rock on top of that hill."

Tom Smith, my great-great-grandfather, told Isabel Kelly that his mother, Tsupu, was "half Petaluma, half Tomales, half Bodega." Despite Tom Smith's problematic math and the fact that no information can be found in mission or church records regarding Tsupu's parents, or, for that matter, for Tsupu herself, one can surmise that it was Tsupu's father who was from Petaluma, since the custom held that women joined the husband's family after marriage. Tsupu later settled in *Eye · kotcha*, or Fruit House, a post–European contact make-shift village in Coleman Valley, in the heart of Bodega Miwok (or Olamentke) territory, where her mother, Tom Smith's grandmother, and his uncles had houses and where Tom Smith was born and grew up. Tsupu's mother more than likely came from Olamentke Nation then, though from which village remains unknown.

Tsupu is the Coast Miwok word for "wild cucumber." A poultice can be made from the plant's juices as an antidote for boils, and the word was sometimes used for "boils" as well as "a cure for boils." Coast Miwok people had many nicknames, and whether or not Tsupu was a nickname or a proper name isn't clear. At some point, she was baptized Maria, and even later was referred to as Maria Checca or Cheka (suggesting Russian influence) and as Maria Chica (suggesting Spanish or Mexican influence). She was also known both as Miss Com-techal and Miss Smith. Ultimately, she had six children and scores of grandchildren and great-grandchildren, and perhaps the many families had as many different names for her. In my family, she was called "Little Grandma." Perhaps she was quite small, shrunken in age, and remembered that way, or maybe she had always been a petite woman.

The relative who told me what little was still known in the family about Tsupu was my father's cousin, who had lived her entire life in East Los Angeles, specifically Boyle Heights, where both she and my father were born after their mothers escaped Sherman Indian School in the 1920s. "Grandma used to talk a little bit about 'Little Grandma,'" my father's cousin said, closing her eyes as if to drown out the noisy street beyond her front door and picture a woman she had never seen, her grandmother's grandmother. It was a hot, uncomfortable afternoon in 1987, and I wanted to go as far back and learn as much about my family history as possible. "Grandma was young when she [Little Grandma] died," my father's cousin added. Then all at once she opened her eyes, looking about the room surprised, as if she had awakened suddenly and found herself back in the old days of Petaluma. She said that when Tsupu died she was wearing her finest clothes, a handmade late-nineteenth-century black dress with a bustle and fitted bodice, and a silk mantilla, popular during the Mexican California period, that covered her face and reached to the ground, as if she had dressed for her own funeral.

She must have been attractive, even beautiful, as she went on to win the heart of Bodega Bay's most important citizen.

When Tsupu was born—by any estimate about 1820—the

village of Petaluma was in crisis. At least a third of its citizens had died within the last ten years of European diseases—smallpox, pneumonia, syphilis—to which the Natives had no resistance; and the great herds of deer and elk, frightened by blasts from Spanish muskets, were scattering, migrating north, replaced by mission livestock—cattle, horses, sheep—which spread foreign seed in dung, giving rise to oatgrass, among other invasive species, that supplanted the native bunchgrasses and sedges. The Lekatuit, like other California aboriginal nations, had had an intimate relationship with their environment, specifically a seasonal schedule of harvesting, pruning, controlled burning, and the like, from which a particular and sustainable ecology had evolved over five thousand years or more. With fewer individuals to tend the landscape or garden, as we liked to call it, and with the major disruption of native animal and plant habitats, the valley began to appear "wild."

Coast Miwok show up on mission records as early as 1786, and in great numbers from 1795 to 1803, but these individuals were largely from southern nations—Huimen, Gualen, and Aguasto. The Spanish made their first incursions into the Petaluma Valley, looking in earnest for Indian recruits for Mission Dolores, in 1814, the year "Petalumas" first appear on mission records. Yet, relatively few "Petalumas" were baptized in the mission; and, later, few "Petalumas" resided in Mission San Rafael, established in 1817 after Spanish soldiers had pushed much farther north into Southern Pomo territory. The Lekatuit, like their Southern Pomo neighbors, were known among the Spanish as "rebellious." No doubt word of mouth from the southern Coast Miwok nations regarding the mistreatment of Indians in the missions impeded the soldiers' attempts to coerce the Lekatuit and Southern Pomo from their villages.

Regardless, the Lekatuit villagers of Petaluma struggled to maintain their traditional lifeways. Tsupu would be schooled by grandparents, as was the custom, and specifically by her grandmother, in this case her father's mother, who was born and came of age in Petaluma before European contact, or at least before European contact created significant change and stress in the village. Tsupu learned basket weaving, including when and where to gather sedge, bulrush, and willow for baskets; she learned when and where to gather acorns, various seeds for pinole, pine nuts, roots, clovers, and over two hundred herbs; she learned how to construct a tule *kotcha*, or house; and she learned how to make women's skirts from tule and how to sew rabbit skins for blankets. She listened to stories. She learned to read the landscape, know its songs, the powers associated with mountains, rocks, streams, an owl's or raven's call, clouds and fog, angles of the sun and moon, and, in the nighttime sky, that shifting map of stars.

Petaluma, like most other Coast Miwok villages, was governed by a nonhereditary headman, known as the *hoipu*, and at least two female leaders, or headwomen, the most powerful of which was known as the *maien*, who, as Tom Smith told Isabel Kelly, "bosses everyone, even hoipu." Anyone, but usually a father, could nominate a young man for the position of hoipu, but a committee of four older women not only made the choice but was responsible for training him in the art of leadership as well, further illustrating the primacy of women in Coast Miwok government. As another example, while men usually hunted important ceremonial birds—woodpeckers, mallards, ravens, condors—it was the women who made the elaborately designed ceremonial capes, skirts, and headdresses with the feathers. Also related to the importance and power of women in the community, rape was unheard of, in part because physical violence was considered the lowest form of power, but also because women were considered to have an abundance of spiritual powers, usually more than men.

Petaluma had two primary subdivisions, or moieties, within the village, known as "Land" and "Water," which correlated with, and hence connected the villagers to, the same two moieties in other Lekatuit villages and Coast Miwok nations. The moieties helped maintain cohesion between nations and were especially important when selecting a marriage partner. After her first menses, when she would have been put in a bed of warm sand for five days, Tsupu was tattooed with slight, zigzagging lines extending from each corner of her mouth to below her chin, indicating not only her village and nation but also her moiety. Tsupu—whether a proper name given thirty days after her birth, or a nickname—is a Land name, and after her first menses she would have been given another Land name, albeit a secret name, perhaps selected by and thus known only to members of a special women's society.

Empowered individuals, Petaluma women were clever and resourceful, and Tsupu must have watched as her grandmother artfully negotiated traditional culture and values amidst Spanish disruption. But neither would escape unscathed the next, and more violent, wave of immigrants.

Missions San Rafael and Solano (in Sonoma) were secularized by the Mexican government in 1834, and Mexican general Mariano Vallejo had already established a military base at Mission Solano a year earlier. Impressed by General Vallejo's military prowess, and anxious to limit Russian expansion from Fort Ross on the north coast, Governor José Figueroa of Monterey rewarded Vallejo title to a ten-league grant known as Rancho Petaluma, about sixty thousand acres stretching from Lekatuit territory in the west to Mission Solano in the east. General Vallejo built his rancho headquarters, an adobe fort, on the grasslands in eastern Lekatuit territory.

The Mexicans established an elaborate slave trade, buying and selling Native men and boys on ranchos, often as far away as Mexico. And Mexican soldiers weren't different from their Spanish predecessors, who, as historian Alan Rosenus notes in *General Vallejo and the Advent of the Americas* (1999), "assumed that the exploitation of Indian women was a right of conquest." Sometime in the first days of the rancho, whether close to its adobe walls or closer to the village of Petaluma, a soldier, or soldiers, found a young girl about fourteen, not a neophyte from the missions in dirty clothing looking for food and work but a Native, barefoot and bare-breasted in a tule skirt, and they hauled her into the fort. What happened there no one knows, nor for how long—days, weeks—she stayed. She did escape, however, having kept an eye open for an unlatched door or a sleeping guard, and began a fifty-mile trek north to Fort Ross, perhaps seeing her village as she passed in the dark of night, her last memory of Petaluma, then a place of shadows.

Tsupu's journey, whether alone or with other escapees, had to have been difficult. More than likely she traveled west from the rancho fort to the coast, following a route she had used many times with other Petaluma villagers to trade with Olamentke villagers for Washington clam shells (used as currency when ground into dime-sized discs), as well as to fish and gather seaweed. And, again, Tsupu's mother had probably come from an Olamentke village, and Tsupu therefore likely had relatives within the coastal villages.

But the trip was still dangerous, as the land was rife with Mexican soldiers, besides those who may have pursued Tsupu, as well as with early Americans, who could surely take advantage of a fourteen-year-old Indian girl defenseless in the brush. Juana Bautista, Maria Copa's mother and the last maien of the Nicasio village, told of being so frightened once at the sound of approaching horses that she lay face down in a dry creek bed and didn't look up, even as she was loaded onto a wagon bed, until she was back at Nicasio several hours later and realized it was her relatives who had picked her up.

After Tsupu forded the Russian River and found herself in Kashaya Pomo territory, following the coastline north toward Fort Ross, the landscape would become increasingly unfamiliar to her. If roving Mexican soldiers and a foreign landscape made the journey dangerous, then so too the animals, particularly grizzly bears, which, like other powerful creatures on the land, no longer enjoyed age-old agreements with humans regarding shared habitats and, thus disrupted and hostile, posed a serious threat to unarmed passersby.

In 1834, Fort Ross was a well-established settlement, Russia's southernmost outpost of a colonial empire that reached from Siberia's Yamal Peninsula. The colony's census indicates nearly a hundred Native women, mostly Kashaya Pomo and Coast Miwok (from Bodega and Jenner), and relatively few Native men, residing at the fort then. Some of the Native men may have been used on boats to scan the coastline for sea otters with the Aleut hunters, who had accompanied the Russian hunters and soldiers to Fort Ross from Alaska, but that is speculation. The greater number of Native women at Fort Ross, however, was almost certainly a result of the needs of the local economy. Native women tended the colony's wheat fields and orchards, and they served as domestics, cooking and washing clothes for its nearly all-male population of foreigners. Kashaya Pomo and Coast Miwok women were also often concubines, if not regular wives, even as they maintained relationships, sometimes tenuously, with their Native husbands, who, because their usefulness around the fort was largely limited to seasonal hunting and fishing, often resided at their respective indigenous villages, quite often raising the mixed-blood children born at the colony.

Indians trapped on Mexican ranchos considered Fort Ross a sanctuary. The Russians, for political reasons, armed the Natives against the Mexicans; and while the Russians expected the Natives to work long hours, they usually did not mistreat them as the Mexicans had. The Russians, members of the Orthodox Church, also weren't interested in converting the Natives, leaving them to their indigenous religious practices.

Because many Native women at Fort Ross were Olamentke, Tsupu no doubt found relatives when she arrived, and certainly women who spoke her language. Apparently, she learned the ropes at the colony rather quickly and not only assumed duties including gardening, washing clothes, tanning hides, and making tallow for soap and candles, but also found a non-resident Native husband with whom she established, as it would turn out, a lasting relationship. His name was Comtechal, a Russian name, or perhaps a Russian pronunciation of an Indian word or name. He was of mixed parentage: his mother was Olamentke, originally from Tókau, a village on the east side of the Bodega peninsula, and his father was "Creole," a Russian term for mixed-blood Natives, in this case a man whose mother was Kashaya Pomo and father half Russian, half Aleut. Even before the Russians abandoned the colony in 1842, Tsupu had left the fort and settled with Comtechal at *Eye · kotcha*, or Fruit House, the makeshift village north of Bodega Bay in Coleman Valley, where they lived with Comtechal's mother and two brothers, and where the last of their three children, Tomás Comtechal, my great-great-grandfather, was born in 1838, hardly four years after Tsupu had left Petaluma.

When the Russians abandoned Fort Ross, after depleting the sea otter population upon which the colony was dependent for pelt trade with China, the Natives were left prey to marauding bands of Mexicans and early American settlers looking for Indian slaves. This was a most horrific period; Indians who were unable to seek protection on Mexican ranches, or as the property of American squatters who "owned" the Indians in exchange for their labor, risked being captured and sold. Comtechal's mother's family had settled at *Eye · kotcha*, probably because of its remote location tucked in the rugged coastal hills and surrounded by gigantic redwoods. But even *Eye · kotcha* must have been threatened as more and more foreigners poured into the region.

Early in 1844, Stephen Smith, an American sea captain from Boston, arrived in Bodega Bay with a 35,787-acre land grant from the Mexican government. He also had with him his fifteen-year-old Peruvian wife, a necessary stipulation of Mexican law, which said that an American must have a "Spanish spouse" in order to obtain a land grant.

Already nearly sixty years old, Captain Smith wasted no time establishing a successful business, if not an empire, in his new home. In 1846 he was appointed the "civil magistrate" for the region by the Mexican government, and that same year, he built in the town of Bodega a sawmill operated by the first steam engine in California. A couple of years later he survived the Bear Flag Revolt, retaining ownership of his sawmill and a large portion of his vast acreage, although at one point during the rebellion, Americans reportedly took some of his horses (which they later returned), and many of the Indians who had previously sought refuge under him fled. But not the young Indian woman from Petaluma—she didn't leave. And the Americans wouldn't touch her. They would no sooner bother her than bother Captain Smith's wife. Everyone knew that Tsupu wasn't mere property, just another concubine. She was the mother of Smith's children, and he loved her.

How Tsupu and Stephen Smith met no one knows. Captain Smith was rumored to have been a good man, kind to the Indians; moreover, he employed them on his rancho

and in his mill, thus affording them both a living and protection from slave traders. Perhaps Tsupu, after a trek from
Eye · kotcha, showed up outside his gate looking for work one
morning, joining the line of Indians that showed up outside
his gate looking for work every morning, and Captain Smith,
needing a housekeeper, picked her out of the line, perhaps
with a couple of other Indian women, and, after taking notice
of her way with an iron and broom, skills she had honed at Fort
Ross, he then saw her actual beauty, maybe heard the sound of
her voice or discovered the way she moved, whatever might
fancy a man, and found he couldn't help himself. Or maybe he
saw her just once, passing on a road or trail, and that was it, his
composure undermined then and there. Whatever the case, it
wasn't long before she was a permanent resident on his rancho, not in any makeshift Indian village or work camp but less
than two hundred feet from his house in his three-story barn,
wherein he had fashioned for her an eight-room home, with a
kitchen, bedrooms, a formal dining room and parlor—all on
polished redwood slab floors. She continued to work, albeit as
a supervisor of housekeepers and gardeners, and this elevated
role may have been what prompted the other Indians to begin
referring to her as maien. After she had children from Smith,
three altogether, he insisted she keep regular help in her home,

and a ninth room, a servant's quarters, was added to the barn.

The first piece of legislation that California enacted after it became a state in 1850 was the Act for the Government and Protection of Indians, which essentially legalized Indian slavery. Captain Smith's Indians, most of whom were Olamentke or who had, like Tsupu, fled north from other Coast Miwok nations, were safe, particularly under the watchful eye not of the captain but of his mistress. While Tsupu's children with Smith stayed at the rancho, her first three children remained at *Eye · kotcha* with their father, Comtechal, but they eventually adopted the name Smith, no doubt for purposes of safety. Hence my great-great-grandfather, Tomás Comtechal, became Thomas, or Tom, Smith. Many local Indians, when approached by American settlers, learned to say their name was Smith, guaranteeing their freedom.

By the time Stephen Smith died in 1855, Tsupu had secured such a position of influence throughout the region that Americans, seeing her approach in horse and buggy, tipped their hats in respect, often confusing her for Smith's actual wife, who rarely left the house. After his death, Tsupu's power didn't wane, partly because she had established a good relationship with Smith's widow, Manuela Torres, who obviously knew of her husband's liaison, having seen the mixed-blood children about the place. Perhaps rather than feel jealous, she had even been relieved by his affections for the Indian woman. Before Manuela left the rancho in about 1870, moving to San Francisco, where she would spend the last year of her life, she made provisions for Tsupu and her family to reside on her late husband's property and even deeded a two-acre plot overlooking Bodega Bay to the "Smith Family" for a cemetery.

Did Tsupu love Captain Smith? The nature of their relationship is no more known than is the manner in which they came together in the first place. What we do know is that she adapted to her new lifestyle within the community. While Tsupu became acquainted with and probably wore Western clothing at Fort Ross, she learned elements of more sophisticated fashion when she got involved with Captain Smith, becoming adept to the extent that, in hats and showy frocks, she dressed to her status as mistress of the most influential man in Bodega. When she met Smith, she already spoke Russian, and she eventually became proficient in Spanish and English as well. But she never forgot her Coast Miwok ways. She wove baskets with designs distinctive of her Petaluma village and Lekatuit Nation; in the hills and gullies, she cut willow branches, and along the creeks she found sedge roots, which she split with her teeth into long, fine strands, necessary for the watertight baskets that fewer and fewer Coast Miwok women could weave. She harvested acorns each fall from under the coastal tanoaks, and even late in her life, she was seen often with a stone pestle pounding acorns into fine meal in a stone mortar or leaching the meal with water over a circular bed of coarse sand. And she never stopped returning to *Eye · kotcha*, not only to see her children there but also Comtechal.

Eventually, the village of *Eye · kotcha* was abandoned, and Comtechal moved to *Tawak · puluk*, or "Shoulder Bone Pond," the location of an ancient Olamentke summer village about three-quarters of a mile north of Bodega Bay. Not long after Manuela moved to San Francisco, Tsupu joined Comtechal at *Tawak · puluk*, in a one-room cabin, and she would remain there for almost thirty years, until he died, two weeks before she died.

Her youngest child with Comtechal, Tom Smith, became the last Coast Miwok medicine man. William Smith, the youngest child of Tsupu and Captain Stephen Smith, built a large house at Bodega Bay, from which his sons established and operated a lucrative fishing business for many years. Today over five hundred individuals trace their ancestry to Tsupu—about the same number of Lekatuit who were living in the ancient village of Petaluma at the time of European contact. One family cousin, Kathleen Smith, a talented artist and descendant of William Smith, demonstrates acorn preparation in Bay Area schools and parks, pounding and leaching acorns as her great-great-grandmother once had with *her* grandmother along the Petaluma River 175 years ago.

Tsupu must've talked about the ancient village. She must've talked about the oak trees and the deer and elk there; maybe she talked about her family, people she knew; and maybe she told the Coyote stories her grandmother had told her. What people remember her saying, what she talked about for the longest time, was the condors, or rather the absence of them. She probably didn't return to the Petaluma Valley until the 1870s, long enough after the Act for the Government and Protection of Indians was repealed that she could travel safely beyond the confines of Captain Smith's rancho. By then the Petaluma region had changed radically: The immense redwood forests on the western hills were gone (Captain Smith clear-cut hills throughout Bodega and as far south as Petaluma), most of the oak groves were gone, what few elk remained in Sonoma County now inhabited an area around the Laguna de Santa Rosa, startled waterfowl didn't obscure the sun, there were farms and a town. Condors, those remarkable creatures with wingspans of up to fourteen feet, whose feathers the Lekatuit used for ceremonial capes and aprons, were last seen in Coast Miwok territory in 1847, when citizens of Fairfax observed "more than a dozen." In 1860, in nearby Contra Costa County, a bird with a wingspan of thirteen and a half feet was spotted. Certainly, Tsupu would have noticed the absence of condors before. But even as her wagon reached the western edge of Petaluma Valley, she mentioned the condors, as if she hadn't until then noticed the empty sky. "How are the people going to dance without feathers?" she asked.

Did she mention the condors on her last trip to Petaluma, when my great-grandmother sat next to her on the wagon? Could she tell as much even though she was blind? Even blind, she knew the route well; perhaps she had made several trips back to Petaluma by then. She died less than a year after that last trip. My father's cousin who told me about Tsupu had told me that she was barefoot, sitting in a chair next to Comtechal's empty pallet, before she died. I see her like that, the last woman of Petaluma, barefoot, in a black dress, a floor-length mantilla already covering her face, sitting certain of the only thing besides her commitment to her children and Comtechal that she wouldn't have to second guess. But my father's cousin would tell me she was certain of something else. On that last trip, after she nodded with her chin to the location of her old village, the family turned the wagon around and then stopped in the town before heading west back to Bodega. "We're in Petaluma," someone informed her. She became indignant. "No," she corrected, "we left it back there."

MARIA
EVANGELISTE

Her name was Maria, which was what the priest at St. Rose Church called all of the Indian girls, even this girl, Maria Evangeliste, who ironed his vestments and each Sunday played the violin so beautifully as the communicants marched to the altar to receive the sacraments that Jesus was said to smile down from the rafters at the dispensation of his body and blood.

That was why on a Friday, when she hadn't returned by nightfall, and by Sunday Mass, when there was still no sign of her, the priest worried as much as her family did, and after Mass notified the sheriff. The flatbed wagon that she had been driving was found by an apple farmer outside his stable, as if the old, pale-gray gelding was waiting to be unhitched and led to a stall inside. The two cherrywood chairs she'd purchased on the priest's behalf stood upright, still on the wagon bed, wedged between bales of straw. The priest had contracted the chairs for his rectory from a carpenter in Bodega; and Maria, needing any small amount of compensation, offered to drive the old gelding a nearly ten-mile trip west and then back. Still, she should have returned before nightfall, for she had left at dawn, the priest's money for the carpenter secure in her coat pocket.

A number of things could've happened to her. The horse might've spooked, jerking the wagon such that if she wasn't paying close attention she would've been tossed to the ground. She might be lying on the roadside someplace, knocked unconscious, a broken back, God forbid a broken neck. She could've been raped, left in the brush somewhere, even. At the time, in 1903, American Indians had not yet been granted U.S. citizenship and therefore had no recourse in a U.S. court. A lone Coast Miwok girl in Sonoma County was easy prey for marauding American men and boys who roamed the back roads, as the old Indians used to say, like packs of dogs.

But wouldn't they have hesitated, considering the possibility that Maria Evangeliste was a U.S. citizen of Mexican descent, a guise many Indians used? Surely, approaching the wagon they would have seen the wooden cross hanging from her neck. If that didn't stop them, she had the ultimate defense, an embroidered crimson sash the priest wore at mass, which he had given her that morning as proof of protection from the Church, and which she'd kept folded in her other pocket, ready in the event someone should assault her, even if only to search her pockets to steal the priest's money for the carpenter. But none of these things happened.

As she rounded a hilly curve on the dirt road, which is now paved and called Occidental Road, she spotted two women. They were Indian women in long nineteenth-century dresses, scarves covering their heads and tied under their chins, and Maria Evangeliste recognized them immediately. They were twin sisters, childless elderly Southern Pomo women from the outskirts of Sebastopol, just a couple miles up the road. They did not resemble one another, one twin short and stout, the other taller, much darker, the color of oak bark. But, at that moment, hardly would Maria Evangeliste have remarked at their appearance, or the fact that, side by side, they stood in the middle of the road halting her passage, or even that she was in the vicinity of the rumored secret cave old people talked about in revered whispers. She understood what was happening without thinking, knew all at once. So when the taller of the two women commanded her off the wagon with only a nod of the chin, she knew she had no choice but to get down and follow them. And, it is told, that was how it started, how the twin sisters took Maria Evangeliste to train her as a Human Bear.

Why Maria Evangeliste was traveling on Occidental Road is a mystery. The usual route from Santa Rosa to the coastal town of Bodega was, and still is, the road west across the lagoon to the town of Sebastopol and then more or less straight to the coast. Returning from Bodega, she would have had to venture north along one of two or three narrow roads, wide paths really, to reach what is now Occidental Road—which would have been a longer, circuitous way to go, not to mention more dangerous given that she would be more isolated in the event she was assaulted. There was also greater risk of the old horse stumbling, some kind of accident with the wagon, on an unreliable road. Did she not want to pass through the town of Sebastopol because it was Friday, late in the day, and gangs of men off work from the sawmill and nearby orchards would already be gathered around the pubs, men who were drinking and might catch sight of her alone? There was an encampment of Indians where Occidental Road emptied onto the Santa Rosa plain—had she a friend she wanted to visit? Winter rain flooded, and still floods, the lagoon—was she traveling at a time when the water was high, when she needed to cross the northern bridge over the lagoon rather than the bridge in Sebastopol?

Following an ancient story of how the Human Bear cult started, in which a lone boy picking blackberries was kidnapped by grizzly bears and afforded their secrets and indomitable physical prowess, it is said that most initiates to the cult were likewise kidnapped. Human Bears might watch a young person carefully for some time, months or even years, regarding the young person's suitability for induction. Stories are told of Human Bears traveling far distances to study a potential initiate, often in the guise of wanting only to see an old friend or to trade. They might even warn chosen individuals of their impending abduction, reminding them that they had no choice henceforth but to acquiesce and keep silent. Had Maria Evangeliste made arrangements beforehand, perhaps driven the priest's wagon north to fulfill her obligation?

Four days later, on a Tuesday morning, she returned to the clapboard house west of town where she lived with her family and a changing assembly of relatives forever in search of work. The small house, said to be owned by a dairy rancher for whom her father worked, sat above Santa Rosa Creek. Behind the house, lining the creek, was a stand of willow trees. A relative of my grandmother's, who first told me this story, said Maria

Evangeliste appeared from behind the trees. Another older relative once pointed to a bald hillside while we were driving on Occidental Road and mentioned the story, claiming that Maria Evangeliste was first discovered standing in front of her house, not coming from behind the willows, and that in the faint morning light she was still as stone. Both versions posit that she was unharmed, returned as she had left, groomed, unsullied.

She could not tell where she had been. Did she lie, perhaps say that she lost control of the wagon after the horse spooked? Did she say as much in order to lead others to believe she'd run off with a young man? What was the sheriff told? The priest? However the case was resolved in the minds of the sheriff and the priest—whether from whatever story the girl might've relayed or from whatever either of them surmised themselves about what happened—the Indians were not so easily satisfied. For the Indians—or at least enough of them to pass on a story, anyway—the girl's answers were suspect and pointed to only one possible outcome: the two old twins in Sebastopol had found a successor.

I visited the bald hillside, parked my car on Occidental Road, then crawled under a barbed wire fence and hiked through brush and looming redwood trees, dark shade. Where would the secret cave be—this side of the hill, below the steep face of naked rock, or around the backside? Would such a cave exist still? Might not loggers or farmers have destroyed it long ago? Unable to see past a thicket of blackberry bramble, I could no longer look back and see the road. The outcropping of rock, exposed above the curtain of treetops, was a face with crater formations and crevices, as if the hill, like an enormous and uninhibited animal, was observing my approach. I became agitated. The story filled me. Oh, these are modern times, I told myself. What's a story these days? If anything, I should be worrying about trespassing on private property. Nonetheless, I stopped. Looking over the blackberry bramble to the trees, I attempted to regain my bearings, again trying to gauge my distance from the road.

In 1903, when the twin sisters abducted Maria Evangeliste, loggers had leveled the trees a second time—or were about to. The magnificent original redwoods, reaching down from the Oregon border to present-day Monterey County, were for the most part cleared between 1830 and 1870. The trees before me, a third growth of redwoods, were about a hundred years old, and a hundred feet tall. In 1903 the gigantic original trees that once sheltered the grizzly bears were gone; and, whether or not the second stand of trees still stood, the grizzly was extinct in the region, killed decades before by Mexican vaqueros and American settlers. The Human Bear cult, like the grizzly bear, was dependent on the trees and on open landscape unencumbered by fences and ranchers protective of livestock. Stories abound—even among local non-Indians—of ranchers felling a bear only to find when they went to retrieve the carcass an empty hide. The twin sisters, how did they instruct their last recruit? Did they show Maria Evangeliste a route that was still safe to travel under a moonless nighttime sky? Did they have only memories to offer, power songs unsung outside the old cave?

Secret societies, such as the Human Bear cult, both perpetuated and reflected Pomo and Coast Miwok worldviews, in which every human, just as every aspect of the landscape, possessed special—and secret—powers. Cult members with their special power and connection to the living world played an integral role in the well-being of the village. Human Bears, assuming the grizzly's strength and extraordinary sense of smell, could locate and retrieve food from far distances. They also possessed "protection," which sometimes consisted of knowledge of a feature of the landscape they might use, such as a cave, but which often was in the form of songs that could cause illness, sometimes death, to anyone who might attempt to harm them. The mere existence of Human Bears would thus make you think twice about harming anyone. Same with a bird, a tree, any tiny stone. Respect becomes the only guarantee of survival. This respect is predicated on remembering that, even with unique power, you are not alone, absolute. As Mabel McKay told me, "Be careful when someone [or something] catches your attention. You don't know what spirit it is. Be thoughtful." The Kashaya Pomo elders refer to Europeans as *pala-cha*, miracles: instead of being punished for killing people and animals, chopping down trees, damming and dredging the waterways, the Europeans just kept coming.

There were numerous secret cults. Many were associated with animals—bobcats, grizzly bears, even birds and snakes. Others were associated with a particular place—a meadow, a canyon, an underwater cave where the spirit of the place empowered its respective cult members. Cults were often gender based: women's Bear cults were considered among the most powerful. In all cases, cult initiates endured long periods of training, not only learning about, for instance, the essentials of their animal powers but simultaneously about the larger environment as well.

Sonoma County, about an hour north of San Francisco, was at the time of European contact one of the most geographically complex and biologically diverse places on earth. Below arid hills, covered with only bunchgrass and the occasional copse of oak and bay laurel, were rich wetlands, inland bays, lakes, a meandering lagoon, and a substantial river and numerous creeks where hundreds of species of waterfowl flew up so thick as to obliterate the sun for hours at a time. Immense herds of elk, pronghorn, and blacktail deer grazed along these waterways on any number of clovers and sedges. West, lining the coastal hills, were redwoods so thick that several yards into a forest all was dark as night. The shifting shoreline, steep cliffs dropping to the water or to broad sandy beaches, was rich too, rife with edible sea kelps and dozens of species of clams, mussels, abalone, and fish—salmon the most prized. Despite these distinct environments—arid hills, lush plains and wetlands, redwood forests—the landscape was usually inconsistent, tricky even. Amidst the arid hills below Sonoma Mountain were numerous lakes and spring-fed marshes.

Meadows, prairie-like, appeared unexpectedly in the otherwise dense and dark redwood forests. A narrow creek might empty into a wide and deep perch-filled pond just on the other side of a small, barren-looking knoll. Traveling through an expanse of marshy plain you might discover, stepping from waist-high sedges, a carpet of rock a mile wide and several miles long, habitat for snakes and lizards that would otherwise be found in the drier foothills. Nothing appeared quite what it seemed. The landscape, complex in design and texture, demanded reflection, study. The culture that grew out of a ten-thousand-year relationship with the place became like it, not just in thought but in deed. Pomo and Coast Miwok art—the most complicated and intricate basketry found among indigenous people anywhere—tells the story.

Human Bears learned the details of the landscape: where a fish-ripe lake hid behind a bend, where a thicket of blackberries loaded with fruit sat tucked below a hillside. At the same time, regardless of their unique ability to travel great distances and seek out food sources for the village, they could not disrespect the hidden lake or thicket of berries, needing always to know the requirements for taking the fish or fruit. The lake had a special—and potentially dangerous—spirit, just as the Human Bear, and so too the blackberry thicket. Developing a heightened sense of the Human Bear's unique power necessitated a heightened sense of the land. Ultimately, the Human Bear cult didn't play an integral role only in the well-being of the village but also, more precisely, in the well-being of the village within the larger world.

By 1903 most of the landscape was transformed. Gone were the vast wetlands. The water table throughout the region had dropped an average of two hundred feet. Creeks went dry in summer. The big trees were gone. Many of the great animals were extinct in the region, not just the grizzly bears but the herds of elk and pronghorn, and the mighty condors gliding the thermals with their fourteen-foot wingspans. Regarding these remarkable ancestral birds, Tsupu, my great-great-great-grandmother, sitting atop a wagon toward the end of the nineteenth century, gazed up at the empty sky and asked, "How are the people going to dance without feathers?" If there was a route safe for Maria Evangeliste to travel as a Human Bear in 1903, would there still exist a familiar bountiful blackberry thicket? An ocean cove where she might collect a hundred pounds of clams?

Just as the landscape was transformed, increasingly so too was the eons-old way of thinking about it. Catholic missionaries put in the minds of Coast Miwok and Pomo villagers the notion of an eternal and spiritual life that was elsewhere, that could not be derived and experienced from the land. The God of an elsewhere kingdom overruled, in fact deemed as evil, anything on the earth that might be considered equally powerful, worthy of reverence and awe. While Christianity was forced upon the Natives, usually under conditions of duress and enslavement, the new religion might have made sense. After European contact, Coast Miwok and Pomo no doubt looked upon the transformed landscape and found that they recognized the place less and less, that, in essence, they were no longer home. Indeed miraculous, the new people could kill animals or level a hill without retribution. Couldn't their one almighty God from another world stop a Human Bear? Yes—seen once as necessary to life and land, a protector of the village, the Human Bear—or anyone who would participate in such things—was now more and more an enemy of our well-being, dangerous at best, possibly evil.

Did Maria Evangeliste know what stories people told about her? If, secretly, she left a cache of ripe fruit or clams outside her home as Human Bears once did in the villages, might she not implicate herself, reveal her secret life, in a world hostile to that life? Wouldn't relatives deem the food the devil's work and toss it out? She was the last Human Bear, they say. When did she stop visiting the cave? When was it over?

The morning she returned she said that she had lost control of the wagon. Or she said she visited a friend and hadn't tied the old gelding well enough. Or she said she met a man. In any event, she went that afternoon with the priest and retrieved the wagon with its still-upright rectory chairs from the apple farmer. And that was how, before sunset, she came back to town, driving the wagon as if nothing was unusual, as if four days had not passed at all. She continued to play violin in the church. She was still entrusted with work for the priest. Sometime later she married a Mexican immigrant. They had eleven children, all of whom lived to adulthood. A great-granddaughter sat next to me in catechism class. The last time I saw her, Maria Evangeliste, that is, was sometime in the early 1970s, about ten years before she died at the age of ninety. I was at a funeral in St. Rose Church. She was in the crowd of mourners, a small Indian woman in a dark dress. She wore a veil, respectfully.

I left town around then and did not return for thirty years. I visited, seeing family, and I came back for tribal business. But I wasn't really back—I wasn't home—which I hadn't yet realized, and didn't understand until later. I wrote about Sonoma County—stories, essays, plays—from memory. In fact, I'd hardly written about anyplace else. But what was I remembering? What did I understand?

Sonoma County had changed dramatically. From the center of what once was small-town Santa Rosa, strip malls and housing developments spread over the vast plain, covering irrigated clover and vetch pastures, fruit orchards and straw-berry fields. Gone, the black-and-white-spotted Holstein cows. Gone, rows of prune and pear trees; the apple orchards north and east of Sebastopol, almost each and every one was routed by grapes: pinot noir, cabernet. The arid foothills are now also covered in grapes—gone, the copses of oak and bay laurel there. Visiting, I noticed these changes; coming home for good, I saw how thorough they were, how far-reaching. Where was my home?

I bought the house on Sonoma Mountain. Bay laurel trees, live oaks, and white oaks surround the house; and, past the trees, there is an expansive view west over vineyard-covered hills and the urban sprawl below, to the Pacific Ocean, which is where at night the web of streetlights stops—and where on a very clear night the full moon lights the sea. That light—that path of moon on the water—was how the dead found their way to the next world, or so our ancestors said. And those same ancestors gathered peppernuts from the six-hundred-year-old bay tree outside my gate. But I was like that—suspended between the old bay tree and the far horizon—as I negotiated what it meant to be home. I hadn't lived on the mountain before. I grew up below, in Santa Rosa.

Then the place remembered me. Stories beckoned. The

dead rose, collected with the living, so that more and more the landscape became a meeting hall of raucous voices. I knew the faces. Not merely my tribal members, as if I was convening a tribal meeting, but the land itself—mountain and plain, oak trees and city lights, birds and animals, Indians and non-Indians, Mexicans, Italians, Blacks, Filipinos, Jews—whomever and whatever I'd known, whomever and whatever I knew, was before me, beckoning. Yes, the dead and the living— how could anything die this way? History, it's no less tangible, palpable, than that grandmother under whose care you found yourself. In a kitchen you have known all your life, with its familiar smells and colors, this grandmother sets a plate of warm tortillas on the table with a bowl of chicken soup and says, "Eat."

Driving here and there, to the university, to the laundromat, the market, here and there with no worry of catching an airplane, seeing this relative or that friend before I left again, I had time, the idleness that accompanies routine, and the old lady with the tortillas and soup was able to catch my attention. Driving over Wohler Bridge west of town—west of Santa Rosa—I glance down and see the riverbank and willows: a bonfire lights a moonless night and Filipino men are gathered around the fire there, and my grandmother, a seventeen-year-old Coast Miwok girl, eyes my grandfather for the first time, a *pinoy* dandy in his pin-striped suit, the big gold watch chain dangling from his breast pocket reflecting firelight, and the bloodletting fighting cocks clashing midair, their tiny silhouettes jumping in his watch glass like a pair of enchanted dancers performing a wild tango my grandmother already wants to learn. From behind the townhouses on Coffey Lane, Holstein cows emerge one by one, full udders swaying, and collect in front of the 7-Eleven where Mrs. Andreoli, forty and soon to be a widow, opens the wooden gate to her milk barn. And Old Uncle, old Pomo medicine man—"don't say his real name"—he's on a bench uptown in Courthouse Square, suspenders and fedora, or he's in his garden behind the fairgrounds, where two hours ago he built a fire below the tall cornstalks and thick gourd vines. Witness as he holds now an ember in the palm of his hand and sees and hears in the orange-red ash "all manner of things": people and animals, songs, old earth rules. Isn't this how some folks saw Maria Evangeliste when she returned on foot after four days to her parents' house?

Years later, when they found themselves next to her, scooping rice in the market or picking prunes in the heat-dusty orchards, didn't they still think and remember?

Here I am not a stranger. Looking back, I see how I'd been a stranger, a newcomer at best, wherever else I had lived. I drove back and forth to the university, to the market, in Los Angeles. I did errands in Manhattan. But it wasn't the same. No stories. No old earth rules. Or, put it this way, I had to learn the stories, listen to the rules as a newcomer, and, like that, as mindful as I could be, make a home. Still, Fifth Avenue mid-day remained less busy for me than a remote redwood grove in Sonoma County. I could be alone in Yellowstone. Or the Grand Canyon. These latter places in particular, beautiful, yes. And solitude. But then what is solitude, however blissful? Can it be experienced except by disengagement from the land's stories, its spirits? Wilderness. The old people said the land became wild after we became separated from it, when there were no longer enough of us to hear its demands and tend to it accordingly. Could Thoreau and Muir experience the land-scape as pristine, and know solitude in it as such, if they knew its stories? If that old woman was there, tortillas and chicken soup at hand, would the land be silent?

At a tribal General Council meeting, I saw Maria Evangeliste's great-grandaughter, the same girl I knew from catechism class. Now approaching sixty, a heavyset woman with a shock of dyed black hair, she sat amidst the sea of faces listening to questions and answers regarding the status of our casino. She looked disgruntled, arms crossed over her chest, face puckered in a scowl, and walked out before the meeting was over, leaving me wondering if she was mad at me or someone else on the council or just at life in general.

Her life, from what I'd heard, hadn't been easy. Five children. Two were in prison. One was dead. Ten grandchildren, five of whom she was raising. Where was the soft-faced, flat-limbed teenager who'd listened with me as Sister Agnes Claire attempted to explain the Holy Ghost?

Some tribal members say I was away too long, that I'd gotten "too white." Did she feel that way about me, that I didn't know my people well enough any longer? Her husband, the father of her five children, was a Mexican immigrant. Did she know that her great-grandfather was a Mexican immigrant also? Had she heard the stories about Maria Evangeliste? Did she care?

Perhaps I write for no other reason than to leave a record for her or anyone besides me who might care, a set of tracks, however faint, down the mountain into the plain and back, connecting to those infinite other pathways that take us and keep us in the land and its life here. But this is what I'm thinking now, as I consider what it means to be a writer here. It wasn't what I was thinking during the meeting seeing Maria Evangeliste's great-granddaughter.

I went to the cave. Driving on Occidental Road, I was quite certain of the spot my cousin had pointed to years before—the bald hillside—if for no other reason than that a hippie commune was there at the time, a settlement of teepees past the redwoods, which I mentioned, prompting from my cousin her story of Maria Evangeliste.

The road curved under a canopy of oak trees and tall pines; four o'clock in the afternoon, autumn, the land was already in shadow, the road lead-gray like the occasional patch of sky above. Human Bears traveled only at night in the pitch black; they did not set out in human form for their caves until late at night either. Secrecy was the initiate's first rule. Mabel McKay once told me of a father up in Lake County who, curious about his daughter's whereabouts at night, unwittingly followed her to a Human Bear cave, whereupon her cult sisters gruesomely murdered him right before her eyes. "Ain't supposed to be seeing them things," Mabel said. "Respect." With this story in mind and the landscape darkening around me, it's no wonder that, past the barbed wire fence and into the trees, I was agitated, so much so that when I looked back and couldn't see the road, I stopped. Respect? Was I disrespecting? These are modern times, I kept telling myself. What's a story these days? Wasn't I curious just to see the cave as a landmark, an outpost of memory? Yes, nothing more. I would leave something, a dollar bill, my handkerchief, out of respect. A lone jay shrieked from somewhere on the other side of the blackberry bramble. I looked up, above the line of trees, to the outcropping of rock, enormous and still watchful, then I left.

It was enough, I told myself. Enough. But I kept thinking of Maria Evangeliste. In the car, driving back to town, my excitement only grew. Past the overreaching branches and thick brush on either side of the road, I saw how a uniform gray light enveloped the land, a color such that everything I could see seemed made from it. I had never seen the light in such a way at that time of day; and, I thought that though Maria Evangeliste, after her first four nights with the twin sisters, emerged and came back to town at dawn, the light and land must have looked this way, new, as she had never seen it before. Then I rounded a curve and, coming down the hill, I saw the broad plain clear to the mountain. City lights shone like tiny flags in the gathering darkness. I pulled over, stopped the car. No, I thought then. After Maria Evangeliste first came out of the cave, it was like this: stories, places—an entire land—that she knew day or night, light or no light, not as if for the first time, but better.

ACKNOWLEDGMENTS

I want to thank Steve Wasserman, Terria Smith, Emmerich Anklam, Lisa K. Marietta, Ashley Ingram, and everyone at Heyday. Thanks also to all my friends and supporters, as well as the elders from whom I have learned so many stories, most notably Mabel McKay.

PUBLICATION HISTORY

"Frost." *News from Native California*, vol. 20, no. 2 (winter 2006/2007).

"Iris." *News from Native California*, vol. 20, no. 3 (spring 2007).

"Osprey." *News from Native California*, vol. 20, no. 4 (summer 2007).

"Scar." *News from Native California*, vol. 21, no. 1 (fall 2007).

"Fidel's Place." *Bay Nature* (July–September 2012), including a special section celebrating the 50th anniversary of Point Reyes National Seashore.

"Bluebelly." *Bay Nature* (January–March 2011). Reprinted in *New California Writing 2012*, edited by Gayle Wattawa (Berkeley: Heyday, 2012).

"The Charms of Tolay Lake Regional Park." *Bay Nature* (July–September 2017).

"Osprey Talks to Me One Day." In *The Russian River and Its Watershed*, by Richard McDaniel (Santa Rosa, CA: Riparianthology Press, 2020). Also in *Wildsam Field Guides* (December 2020).

"After the Fall." *Los Angeles Times*, April 2005.

"The Ancient Ones." In *The Once and Future Forest* (Berkeley: Heyday; and San Francisco: Save the Redwoods League, 2019).

"The Last Woman from Petaluma." In *Celebrating Petaluma* (Petaluma, CA: Petaluma Sesquicentennial Committee, 2009). Republished online by KCET—KCETLINK Media Group, September 29, 2016, https://www.kcet.org/shows/tending-the-wild/the-last-woman-from-petaluma.

"Maria Evangeliste." In *West of 98: Living and Writing the New American West*, edited by Lynn Stegner and Russell Rowland (Austin, TX: University of Texas Press, 2011). Reprinted in *New California Writing 2013*, edited by Gayle Wattawa and Kirk Glaser (Berkeley: Heyday, 2013).

ABOUT THE AUTHOR

Greg Sarris is currently serving his sixteenth term as Chairman of the Federated Indians of Graton Rancheria and his first term as Board Chair for the Smithsonian's National Museum of the American Indian. He is also a member of the Board of Regents of the University of California. His publications include *Keeping Slug Woman Alive* (1993), *Mabel McKay: Weaving the Dream* (1994, reissued 2013), *Grand Avenue* (1994, reissued 2015), *Watermelon Nights* (1998, reissued 2021), *How a Mountain Was Made* (2017, published by Heyday), and *The Forgetters* (2024, published by Heyday). Greg lives and works in Sonoma County, California. Visit his website at greg-sarris.com.